Marcia Nelson
118 Falconer St
Frewsburg N.Y.

Southern Living® Cookbook Library

The
Quick and Easy
Cookbook

Copyright© 1972 Oxmoor House, Inc.
All rights reserved.
Library of Congress Catalog Number: 76-41573
ISBN: 0-8487-0335-9

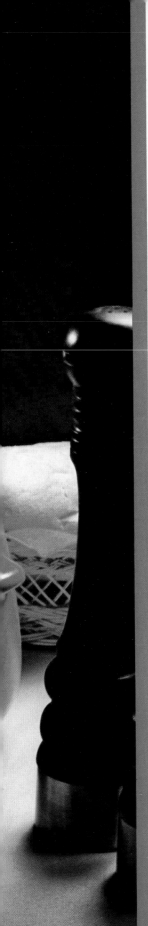

Cover: White Beans in Tomato Sauce (page 101)

Left, Clockwise from top: Fruit Compote (page 166),
Melba Peach Salad (page 30), Shrimp Jambalaya (page 39),
Red Snapper with Corn Bread Stuffing (page 94), Sweet
Potatoes with Meringue Topping (page 115)

contents

Boneless Turkey Roll (page 79)
Fresh Vegetable Kabobs (page 117)

preface

Have you ever wished that someone would prepare a cookbook especially for use on those all-in-a-rush days . . . days when club meetings, car pool duties, or the pressure of a job prevent your preparing the kinds of meals you'd like to serve your family?

Well, wish no more! With the Southern Living Cookbook Library's *Quick and Easy Cookbook*, your problems are over. In the information-packed pages of this book, you'll find suggestions for preparing almost-instant dishes in every food category. Appetizers and sandwiches . . . salads and soups . . . meats . . . poultry . . . seafoods . . . vegetables . . . casseroles . . . egg and cheese dishes . . . desserts . . . breads — a wide variety of favorite foods are highlighted in these easy-to-prepare recipes.

In fact, this useful cookbook features hundreds of home-tested, family-approved recipes which can be prepared and served in just minutes. Every recipe is the favorite of a southern homemaker who knows she can depend on her recipe . . . and so can you!

To help you save more time in the kitchen, this book also features special sections giving hints for quick and easy cooking . . . tips on creating a timesaving kitchen . . . and a list of foods to keep on your pantry shelf for emergency meals. From our kitchens to yours, welcome to the wonderful world of quick and easy cooking — southern style!

Is there a magical secret to carefree cookery? Probably not, but at least three elements play important roles in quick and easy food preparation. One is *advance planning.* Know the foods you have on hand and how you plan to use them — you'll save hours when you don't have to pick up a little of this or a bit of that to prepare your meals. Have a special shelf of emergency foods — condensed, canned, or dried foods you can prepare in a jiffy whenever the need arises. There's a special section on pages 12 and 13 to help you stock such a shelf. The second element is *reliable recipes* for quick and easy foods — and that's what this book is all about.

The third element is *tricks of the homemakers' trade* — the little hints and secrets passed on by one generation of women to another, all with one purpose: to save time in the kitchen. In this section, a collection of such hints has been assembled and classified under the food types they relate to.

special hints

FOR QUICK AND EASY COOKING

The italicized words at the beginning of each hint will help you find just the one you need in seconds.

SOUPS AND STEWS

Make soup stock with the help of your pressure cooker. Bones and scraps of meat should be placed in a cooker filled slightly less than half with water. Cook at 15 pounds of pressure for 15-30 minutes, and the result will be a highly concentrated broth.

Soup stocks may be frozen by placing them in ice cube trays and freezing. When they have set, pop them out of the trays into freezer bags, and store in your freezer. If you follow directions for the stock described above, or if you freeze stock left over from roasting or baking, you'll use one or two cubes to a cup of water to yield a serving of flavorful broth. Or these handy cubes can be used to help strengthen and stretch gravies, vegetable or meat soups, and stews.

To remove fat from soup stock, float a large lettuce leaf on top of the liquid. Remove leaf when it has absorbed fat. Repeat as often as necessary to remove all fat. This method is less time-consuming than the traditional one of placing stock in the refrigerator and skimming off cooled fat.

When cooking dumplings on top of soups or stews, replace the metal lid of your saucepan with a tightly-fitting glass pie plate. The clear plate will let you see when the dumplings are done without having to waste your time lifting the lid. And every time you uncover your saucepan, you must then wait for the steam to reform before the cooking process can continue.

SALADS

When washing salad greens, always lift them away from the water — the sand and grit will wash down into the water, saving you the trouble of repeated washings.

Save time mixing dressing by assembling the ingredients in the bottom of your salad bowl. Cross the salad fork and spoon above the ingredients, pile greens on top of the utensils. Then when you toss the salad, you'll be mixing the dressing as well. And you only have one bowl at clean-up time.

For quick salad dressings, add juice of half a lemon to a cup of yogurt or sour cream. Blend well and add salt and pepper to taste; add crumbled bleu cheese to French dressing; combine thin honey with bottled lime juice to taste; mix mayonnaise with orange juice.

BREADS

For individual slices of seasoned bread, butter French bread slices and season them with garlic, onion, or seeds. Freeze the slices on a cookie sheet, then remove the slices to a plastic bag and return them to the freezer. You'll have individual slices of seasoned bread available whenever you need them — and they won't stick to one another.

For instant canapes, separate a package of refrigerator biscuits, split them, and to each half add half an anchovy fillet or a whole smoked oyster. Fold biscuit over seafood and seal edges. Brush tops with oil from fish can; bake at 450 degrees for 12 minutes.

For quick pizzas, flatten individual refrigerator biscuits, top with pizza makings, and bake at 450 degrees until cheese melts and biscuits are browned.

In preparing homemade bread, look for recipes using the "batter method" — you mix the dough in a bowl with an electric mixer, pour it into greased pans, and let rise once. It cuts your time in less than half, and still allows you to serve your family great homemade bread.

VEGETABLES

When heating canned vegetables, remove the lid, set the can in a pan of water filled to one-half the depth of the can, cover the pan, and cook. In no time at all, the food is hot and ready to serve, and you have eliminated time-consuming clean-up afterwards!

Cook fresh asparagus in your coffee maker (after removing the interior works). You will use little water and the spears will not become bruised from moving around.

Remember frozen vegetables — they cook in about ten minutes and taste delicious with a touch of herbs and spices. And *frozen seasonings* such as chive or onion are easy to use.

Add flavor excitement in seconds by sprinkling butter with your favorite herbs, then melting over vegetables — the butter will coat the vegetables, creating an instant herb-flavored butter sauce.

When husking fresh corn, remove the silk which clings to the kernels by wiping the entire ear with a dampened paper towel. It cleans like magic!

To peel tomatoes easily, dip them in boiling water, then in cold — or rub the tomato skin with the back of a table knife. Then peel the skin with a sharp knife.

To cook frozen vegetables in the oven, remove the frozen block from its package and place it on a square of foil. Put two pats of butter on top and season with salt, pepper, and herbs, if desired. Fold foil over and tightly seal, leaving room inside the package for steam expansion. Bake at 425 degrees for 30 to 40 minutes — no messy pans and no time-consuming watching to be certain the water doesn't evaporate!

For a gourmet asparagus-ham supper, roll four stalks of cooked asparagus in a thin slice of boiled ham and fasten with a toothpick. Place under the broiler three inches from the heat for five minutes. Turn, and broil for another five minutes. Top with cheese sauce, and serve.

FRUITS

A fruit compote makes a beautiful dessert and can be prepared in just minutes. It's a great way to use up leftover fruit, too. Mix the fruit pieces gently, being careful not to bruise them. Serve with their mingled syrups or add a hint of your favorite liqueur. Delicious!

Peel fruits with a stainless steel knife to avoid discoloration; use a vegetable peeler to save time and to preserve many nutrients which lie just under the skin.

Keep a stock of citrus fruit peel on hand. When a recipe calls for citrus fruit juice, grate the rind and store it in your refrigerator in a tightly covered jar. It's ready to use when you need it!

MEATS, SEAFOOD, POULTRY

Devein shrimp quickly and easily by using a bottle opener. Zip the point down the vein canal, and the job is done!

Make meat loaves by baking them in metal juice cans — either the large ones or the smaller, frozen juice cans. The latter make meat loaves just the right size for individual servings, or slice for sandwiches or party canapes. And if you prepare a double recipe, you can store half in the freezer for those meal-time emergencies we all have to face! Best of all, cooking in juice cans prevents a messy, greasy roasting pan which has to be cleaned up.

Freeze meat slices on a cookie sheet, and after freezing, place them in plastic bags. They will not stick together. This same hint works with hamburgers, too.

Prevent bacon from curling by placing the bottom of a pan on top of the slices as they cook.

For an easy corned beef supper, chill a can of corned beef hash. Remove both ends of the can, and push the meat out. Cut it into rounds, and place them under the broiler three inches from heat for seven minutes. Turn, and spread each round with mild horseradish. Top with a tomato slice and sprinkle with grated cheese. Broil five minutes more, and serve.

Use bottled salad dressings as marinades for meat, seafood, and poultry.

A fast and fancy marinade for poultry is made by mixing two tablespoons of lemon juice with one-quarter cup of salad oil and adding a teaspoon of dried tarragon. Use this marinade to baste broiling chicken, and the result is a gourmet's delight.

For a quick ham bake, brown a one-half inch thick ham slice and cut it in half. Place each half on a square of foil and top with a pineapple slice, candied cherry, and one tablespoon brown sugar. Fold package tightly and place on baking sheet. Bake at 425 degrees for 30 minutes.

DESSERTS

Make sugar cookies effortlessly by rolling out your dough on a surface covered with a half-and-half mixture of flour and sugar. As you lift off the cutout cookies, turn them so that the sugared side faces up when they are on the cookie sheet. Not only are they perfectly sugared, but you aren't confronted with the problem of cleaning a cookie sheet which has been liberally sprinkled with sugar!

To have instant cookies on busy days, make a double batch of dough when you have time to prepare it. Bake what you need and place the rest in frozen fruit juice cans which have the tops removed but the bottoms intact (pack them tightly). Then refrigerate the dough-filled cans. When you want to bake cookies in just a few minutes, take out one of these cans, remove the bottom end, and push the dough out, slicing it into quarter-inch slices. Place cookies on a sheet and bake as recipe directs.

Make quick frostings for your cakes by using candy bars. As soon as the cake comes from the oven, place peppermint patties, chocolate bars, or even marshmallows on the warm surface (to within half an inch of the edge). Let the candy melt, and spread it with a knife.

Fast and fancy pastries can be made with prepackaged dough. Roll it paper thin, top with cinnamon and sugar (or other combinations of spices and sugar), and slice into strips about an inch wide. Cut each strip into two-inch pieces; place four pieces one on top of the other, and bake at 425 degrees until brown. This napoleon-like pastry is delicious topped with whipped cream or ice cream!

What's the key to quick and easy kitchen management? It's organization, of course. If you want to take a giant step toward a kitchen that's effortless to work in, *clean out.* Harden your heart and put away — or give away — all those extra spoons, knives, and utensils you've held onto because you might need them someday. If you haven't used them in the last year, chances are you're not going to. Once you have cleaned house, you'll have lots of space you can use to organize utensils so that they're easy to locate.

TIMESAVING EQUIPMENT

There are certain pieces of equipment essential to maintaining a good quick and easy cooking style. Prominent among them are two major kitchen appli-

TIMESAVING
kitchen hints

ances: the blender and the pressure cooker. *The blender* helps you prepare a myriad of dishes. It can be used to grate stale dried cheese for a quick and easy casserole topping. It's invaluable for breaking up lumpy brown sugar and for restoring the silky texture of leftover gravies and sauces. Begin with one-half cup of gravy or sauce in the blender, and gradually add the remainder, blending until smooth. Or use the blender to make your own bread crumbs. Break pieces of stale or toasted bread that has been buttered into the blender container. Blend on low speed for medium crumbs, and on high for fine crumbs.

A pressure cooker will enable you to cook a hot, nourishing and flavorful meal in just minutes. Check the manufacturer's recommendations for using your cooker, and follow them completely. Any do-it-yourself variations almost always ensure trouble. Most soups are prepared under 15 pounds of pressure; meats are cooked at lower pressure, usually about four pounds. Low pressures should be used when cooking fresh fruits or vegetables; frozen ones may be cooked at higher pressures. Follow the cooking tips which accompany your cooker, and you'll be amazed at the time you save. One hint: season with a light touch — less seasoning is needed in pressure cookery than in the regular methods.

In addition to the two pieces of equipment described above, you'll also enjoy the convenience of a *portable electric beater* and *toaster oven.* Add to that such utensils as a *grater, wire whisk, garlic press, kitchen scissors, food tongs, vegetable parer, slotted spoon,* and *rubber spatula.* Then, you'll have the basic utensils for quick and easy cooking.

There are some other things you'll want to have on hand, too, such as *plastic wrapping* (both in rolls and bags of at least two sizes); *a cutting board; kitchen knives* for paring, chopping, and slicing; a *knife sharpener;* various sizes of *glass jars* with tight screw tops; *a fondue set* (pot, burner, tray, and long-handled forks); and a *charcoal grill.*

TIMESAVING TIPS

When a recipe for sauces or custards calls for scalded milk, use cold milk instead. It blends just as well with less danger of curdling. A smoother product is the result, and you save the time you'd spend scalding milk and cleaning up the pan.

Butter or margarine is easy to measure if you buy packages containing quarter-pound sticks. One stick is the equivalent of half a cup or eight tablespoons. Just cut, and use — no time-consuming measuring.

Save dishwashing time when cooking. Measure dry ingredients first, place them on a sheet of waxed paper, then use the same cup to measure liquids.

Plan ahead. When you bring home a piece of cheese and need a small amount of it grated, grate the whole wedge or block then and there. Store the excess in a tightly-covered jar to keep until you use another recipe that calls for grated cheese. No more time-consuming grating until your excess stock runs out!

When you bake a casserole, double the recipe and freeze half. In a short-of-time emergency, imagine how nice it will be to pull out a ready-to-cook casserole from your freezer.

Don't overlook the possibilities of seasonings. They can often make the difference between drab quick cookery and that which reflects imagination and verve. Experiment with herbs and spices — and top foods with seasoned butters. Dress up the foods you serve with a quick sprinkling of paprika, parsley, chive, or add a hint of poppy, caraway, or sesame seeds.

Use plastic bags whenever possible. The large ones hold foods for the freezer, salad greens fresh from the market (already washed, dried, torn, and ready for tossing), cut vegetables, breads of all kinds — even extra ice cubes at party time. Small bags hold everything from individual portions of meat, seafood, or poultry to be frozen or stored to leftovers, grated cheese, or bread crumbs.

Use aluminum foil to cover a dish which is browning too quickly, to hold sifted flour, grated cheese, or bread crumbs; to provide a mixing surface for cinnamon and sugar; to cover your oven racks and provide an impromptu (and disposable) cookie sheet; to cover your broiler and save precious minutes of cleaning up time.

Throughout this book, the concept of advance planning has been emphasized. One major part of planning ahead is the emergency shelf — that shelf of your cupboard set aside for foods you will use in preparing quick and easy meals. The list of suggested foods you'll find on these pages is just that — a list of suggestions. You'll want to add your own favorites and those foods called for in your most depended-upon recipes. But use this list as a basic guide.

Soups. Canned soups are a boon for today's busy homemaker. Plan to stock the flavors listed below along with others that are your family's favorites.

Cream of chicken	Tomato
Cream of celery	Consomme
Cream of mushroom	Cheddar cheese

a pantry shelf

FOR EMERGENCY MEALS

Meats. The many kinds of canned meats offer every homemaker a variety of main dishes for quick and easy meals. Many of them can go into casseroles or provide the basis of sandwich fillings. Plan to stock:

Ham	Prepared meat salads
Chicken (boned as well as	Pressed meat (Spam, etc.)
with dumplings)	Corned beef hash
Potted meats	

Fish. Like canned meat, canned fish can be an invaluable aid when you're confronted with the need to prepare a meal in a minute. You'll want to keep on hand at least one can each of:

Salmon	Shrimp
Tuna fish	Sardines
Lobster	Oysters
Crab	

Fruits. For versatility and good flavor, fruits are difficult to beat. Be certain that your shelf includes:

Fruit cocktail	Cherries
Peach halves	Applesauce
Pear halves	

Vegetables. Every meal needs a vegetable dish for color, flavor, and texture contrast. You can be certain of having sufficient vegetables to meet the needs of every emergency meal when you keep on hand a supply of:

Tomatoes (whole pack, puree, sauce, and paste)	Asparagus
	Beets
Onions (tiny whole)	Beans (limas, baked, string, kidney)
Carrots	Green peas
Corn (both cream and whole kernel)	

Starches. The foods in this group are often used as the basis of in-a-hurry pantry shelf casseroles or as extenders for leftovers. They're invaluable, and you'll want to keep in stock:

Potatoes (instant mashed and tiny whole)	Macaroni
Rice (both brown and white types, quick-cooking)	Noodles (small ones for stroganoff and other similar dishes and the wider ones used for lasagna)
Spaghetti	

Bread mixes. These are a must for plan-ahead homemakers. Include the following kinds on your emergency shelf:

Biscuit mix	Corn bread mix
Pancake mix	Muffin mix

You'll also want to include crackers (soda, fancy round, flavored, snack-type, and oysterettes) and melba toast.

Desserts. The kinds and varieties of mixes available today encourage every homemaker, even when her time is shortest, to finish her meal with a special fillip. Basic emergency dessert supplies include:

Puddings (both instant and canned)	Prepared pie crusts
Cake mix	Frosting mix
Pie crust mix	Cookie mix

Miscellaneous. This category includes accompaniments and complementary foods you'll want to keep a handy supply of on your shelf:

Pimentos	Spaghetti sauce mix
Olives	Gravy mixes
Mushrooms	Bread crumbs
Milk (canned evaporated, powdered)	Lemon juice
Cream substitute	Pickles
Mayonnaise	Salad dressing mix
Nuts (walnuts, pecans, almonds)	

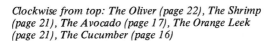

*Clockwise from top: The Oliver (page 22), The Shrimp
(page 21), The Avocado (page 17), The Orange Leek
(page 21), The Cucumber (page 16)*

appetizers &
sandwiches

Appetizers and sandwiches are great friends of today's extra-busy homemakers. Flavorful, eye-appealing appetizers give family and friends a little something to assuage their hunger while you whip up an almost-instant meal. And sandwiches are so marvelously versatile, they become the center of attraction at snack- or party-time, suppers, lunches — on every meal occasion!

This section brings together the most flavor-filled appetizer and sandwich recipes southern homemakers have created. The next time you need appetizers in minutes, turn to these pages and discover home-tested, highly-acclaimed recipes for Garlic-Cheese Straws ... Golden Crown Pate ... Ham and Chicken in Cranberry Sauce ... Crab in Mushrooms ... Stuffed Cucumber Rings ... and other equally delicious appetizers. Only you will know how easy they are to prepare!

And when someone in your family arrives home with a gang of hungry people, don't panic. The sandwich recipes you'll find in the following pages will satisfy even the heartiest eaters — and they take just minutes to prepare. Combine two of everyone's popular foods and serve Ham-Cheese Crunch Sandwiches. There's even a recipe for exotic Hawaiian Sandwiches!

Yes, when you want fast but fabulous sandwiches or appetizers, turn to these pages. You'll find everything you need here!

Cheesy Tuna-Onion Fondue (below)

CHEESY TUNA-ONION FONDUE
Easily prepared in 20 minutes

1 env. dry onion soup mix
2 c. milk
1 lb. process American cheese,
   shredded
3 tbsp. chopped parsley

1 7-oz. can tuna in vegetable
   oil, drained, flaked
Unsalted crackers
Corn chips
Potato chips

Mix the dry soup and milk in a medium saucepan and cook over low heat until almost to boiling point. Add a small portion of the cheese and stir constantly until the cheese is melted. Add cheese gradually, stirring constantly, melting each addition. Add the parsley and tuna. Turn into a fondue saucepan and partially cover flame to keep the tuna mixture just warm. Dip with crackers and chips. 4-6 servings.

THE CUCUMBER
Allow 30 minutes for marinating; assemble in 10 minutes

2 cucumbers
1 1/2 tsp. salt
6 slices whole wheat bread
6 tbsp. soft butter
3 hard-cooked eggs, sieved

12 canned pitted California
   ripe olives, halved
Sour Cream Whip
Sliced green onion

Peel the cucumbers, then slice very thinly and sprinkle with salt. Chill for at least 30 minutes, then squeeze out the excess moisture. Spread the bread with butter, then arrange the cucumbers, sieved eggs and halved ripe olives on the bread. Top with Sour Cream Whip and sprinkle with the green onion. Eat with a knife and fork, spreading the whip over top. 6 open sandwiches.

Sour Cream Whip

3/4 c. sour cream	1 tbsp. thinly sliced green onion
1 tbsp. lemon juice	1/2 tsp. salt

Combine all the ingredients and blend well.

Photograph for this recipe on page 14.

THE AVOCADO
Preparation and cooking time less than 30 minutes

1/2 c. soft butter	12 cherry tomatoes, halved
1 tbsp. crumbled basil	12 canned pitted California
6 slices corn bread	ripe olives
6 slices bacon	Salt and pepper to taste
1 ripe avocado, sliced	1 lime

Mix the butter and basil and spread over the corn bread. Cut the bacon slices in half and fry until crisp. Arrange the bacon strips, avocado, tomato halves and ripe olives on the cornbread, then sprinkle with salt and pepper. Cut the lime into sixths and garnish each sandwich with a wedge. Lime juice may be squeezed over all sandwich ingredients. Serve with a knife and fork. 6 open sandwiches.

Photograph for this recipe on page 14.

GARLIC-CHEESE STRAWS
Elegant but quickly prepared; 12 minutes for baking

1/2 c. shortening	3 tbsp. grated Parmesan cheese
1 c. grated sharp American	3/4 tsp. garlic salt
cheese	1 c. sifted flour

Cream the shortening in a bowl. Add the cheeses and mix well. Sift the garlic salt and flour together and stir into the creamed mixture. Mix until smooth and place in a cookie press with a flat sawtooth tip. Press in 5-inch lengths on an ungreased cookie sheet. Bake at 350 degrees for 12 minutes. Cool for several minutes and remove from cookie sheet carefully.

Helen Janis Hale, Somerset, Kentucky

CHAMPAGNE-CHEESE SPREAD
Elegant but quickly prepared

1/2 lb. mellow Gorgonzola	Cayenne pepper to taste
cheese	3/4 c. champagne
1/4 lb. butter, softened	

Blend the cheese and butter to a smooth paste. Add the cayenne pepper and stir in the champagne. Serve with crackers or small squares of toast.

Mrs. Milton Rodolphe, Greensboro, North Carolina

CHEESE CARROTS
Prepare ahead; chill until serving time

1 3-oz. roll nippy cheese	4 drops of Worcestershire
1/3 c. grated carrot	sauce
1/4 tsp. salt	1 tbsp. chopped onion
Dash of cayenne pepper	Parsley sprigs

Mix the cheese and carrot. Add the salt, cayenne pepper, Worcestershire sauce and onion and mix well. Roll into miniature carrot shapes and chill until firm. Add a small sprig of parsley to top of each carrot.

Mrs. Jean Yarbrough, Knoxville, Tennessee

FROMAGE BALL
Partially prepared ahead; allow 10 minutes to complete

1 8-oz. package cream	White pepper to taste
cheese	2 tbsp. grated onion
1/2 lb. sharp Cheddar cheese,	2 tbsp. chopped pimento
grated	2 tbsp. Worcestershire sauce
1/2 lb. American cheese,	1/2 tsp. soy sauce
grated	1/2 tsp. hot sauce
2 tbsp. chopped green pepper	3/4 c. finely chopped
Pinch of salt	pecans

Soften the cream cheese in a bowl. Add the grated cheeses and mix well. Add remaining ingredients except pecans and mix well. Form into a large ball and wrap in foil. Store in refrigerator for at least 2 days. Roll in pecans.

Mrs. Kay Fulton, Farmington, Arkansas

GOLDEN CROWN PATE
Prepare ahead; chill until serving time

1 env. unflavored gelatin	1 8-oz. package cream cheese
1 10 1/2-oz. can consomme	12 oz. liver pate

Soften the gelatin in 1/4 cup consomme. Heat remaining consomme to boiling point, then stir in the gelatin until dissolved. Combine the cream cheese, liver pate and enough heated consomme mixture for thick spreading consistency. Pour remaining consomme mixture into a crown mold and chill until firm. Spread cream cheese mixture over top and chill. Serve with bread rounds or crackers. 10-15 servings.

Mrs. J. L. Jones, Johnson City, Tennessee

MAUNA KEA SAUSAGES
Elegant but quickly prepared; allow 10 minutes to heat

1 med. green pepper	2 8-oz. packages hot
1 13 1/2-oz. can pineapple	brown-and-serve sausage
chunks	links

4 tsp. cornstarch
1/2 tsp. salt
1/2 c. maple-flavored syrup
1/3 c. water

1/3 c. vinegar
1/2 c. drained maraschino
   cherries

Cut the green pepper in 3/4-inch squares. Drain the pineapple and reserve 1/2 cup syrup. Cut the sausage links in thirds crosswise and brown in a skillet. Blend the cornstarch, salt, reserved syrup, maple-flavored syrup, water and vinegar in blazer pan of chafing dish and heat to boiling point over medium heat, stirring constantly. Cook and stir for several minutes longer. Add the pineapple, sausage, green pepper squares and cherries and heat through. Keep warm over hot water. Spear with cocktail picks. About 150 appetizers.

Mrs. Lawrence Owings, Pine Bluff, Arkansas

EGG AND CHICKEN LIVER CANAPE
20 minutes to prepare

6 lge. chicken livers
2 sm. onions, sliced
Butter
6 hard-cooked eggs

2 tbsp. mayonnaise
1 1/2 tsp. catsup
Onion salt and pepper
   to taste

Saute the livers and onions in small amount of butter in a skillet until tender, then place in a bowl. Add the eggs and mash all ingredients. Stir in the mayonnaise, catsup, onion salt and pepper. Spread on party rye bread or crackers. 6 servings.

Mrs. B. Brown, Birmingham, Alabama

SAUSAGE BALLS
Prepare ahead; allow 30 minutes to reheat and serve

2 lb. hot bulk sausage
1/2 c. catsup
1/2 c. wine vinegar

1/2 c. (packed) brown sugar
1 tbsp. soy sauce
1/2 tsp. ginger

Shape the sausage into small balls. Fry in a skillet over low heat until well done, then drain on paper towels. Combine remaining ingredients in a saucepan and heat through. Add the sausage and stir gently until all of the balls are coated. Cool. Refrigerate for at least 24 hours. Reheat to serve. May be refrigerated for 4 to 5 days or frozen. 40-50 cocktail servings.

Mrs. Frank Parke, Portsmouth, Virginia

TANGY LIVER PATE
Prepare ahead; chill until serving time

1/2 lb. liverwurst
1/2 c. mayonnaise
2 tbsp. chopped parsley

2 tbsp. grated onion
Dash of pepper

Mash the liverwurst in a bowl and blend in mayonnaise, parsley, onion and pepper. Cover and chill. Spread on crackers. 1 1/2 cups.

Mrs. Charles Nichols, Corpus Christi, Texas

Shrimp Salad Boats (below)

SHRIMP SALAD BOATS
Prepare ahead; chill until serving time

2 lb. fresh or frozen shrimp	24 poppy seed rolls
2 c. diced celery	Butter
1/2 c. mayonnaise	Chopped fresh or freeze-dried
Salt and pepper to taste	chives

Shell and devein the shrimp. Cook according to package directions, then drain and chill. Cut 12 shrimp in half lengthwise and chop the remaining shrimp. Mix with the celery and mayonnaise and season with salt and pepper, then chill. Slice the rolls almost through, leaving a hinge. Spread with butter and sprinkle with chives. Fill each roll with a heaping tablespoon of shrimp salad and garnish with a shrimp half. Wrap and chill until serving. 24 sandwiches.

SHRIMP SWEDE
Prepare ahead; chill until serving time

2 lb. fresh or frozen shrimp	3 tbsp. chili sauce
1/2 c. shrimp and crab boil	Dash of salt
3 sm. cans water chestnuts	Pepper to taste
1/2 c. sour cream	Paprika
3 tbsp. horseradish	Parsley sprigs

Place the shrimp in a saucepan and cover with boiling water. Add the shrimp and crab boil and cook over low heat until shrimp turn pink. Drain. Place in ice water and peel and devein. Refrigerate in a covered dish. Drain the water chestnuts and slice medium thin. Refrigerate in a covered dish. Combine the sour cream, horseradish, chili sauce, salt and pepper and blend well. Refrigerate. Spear a shrimp and a slice of water chestnut on a colored toothpick and place on a tray. Repeat with remaining shrimp and water chestnut slices. Top each with a dollop of sour cream mixture and add dash of paprika and sprig of parsley. 12 servings.

Mrs. Virginia C. Lee, Memphis, Tennessee

THE SHRIMP
Partially prepared ahead; assemble at serving time

1/2 lb. cooked, peeled and deveined shrimp	1/2 8-oz. package cream cheese
Dry sherry	12 canned pitted California ripe olives
3 tbsp. lemon juice	
4 slices light rye bread	2 tbsp. chopped parsley
3 tbsp. soft butter	Pepper to taste

Toss the shrimp in 3 tablespoons sherry and the lemon juice, then let stand for 30 minutes. Spread the bread with butter. Soften the cream cheese at room temperature, then mix with 2 teaspoons sherry, then spread on the buttered bread. Drain the shrimp and cut the ripe olives in half, then arrange over the cream cheese. Sprinkle the parsley and pepper over the top. 4 open sandwiches.

Photograph for this recipe on page 14.

THE ORANGE LEEK
Preparation time less than 30 minutes

6 tbsp. soft butter	9 canned pitted California ripe olives, quartered
2 1/2 tsp. ground coriander	
3 slices dark unseeded rye bread	1 orange, peeled and thinly sliced
1 7-oz. can tuna, drained	3 tbsp. thinly sliced leeks

Mix the butter and coriander and spread over the bread. Arrange the flaked tuna, quartered olives, sliced orange and leeks on the bread. 3 open sandwiches.

Photograph for this recipe on page 14.

HOT CRAB MEAT SPREAD
Easily prepared; allow 10 minutes for baking

1 8-oz. package cream cheese	1 can crab meat, drained
3 tbsp. milk	Paprika or slivered almonds to taste (opt.)
1 tsp. minced onion	
1 tsp. cream-style horseradish	Crackers or sm. rye bread slices

Soften the cream cheese. Add the milk and mix well. Add the onion and horseradish. Flake the crab meat and stir into cream cheese mixture. Place in a small baking dish and sprinkle paprika on top. Bake at 350 degrees for 10 minutes or until heated through. Serve with crackers.

Mrs. Ben W. Fisher, Dallas, Texas

CRAB IN MUSHROOMS
Fancy, yet easy to prepare; allow 20 minutes for cooking

1 lb. large fresh mushrooms	1 7 1/2-oz. can crab meat
Melted butter or margarine	1/2 c. sour cream
3 tbsp. fine dry bread crumbs	1/2 c. mayonnaise or salad
2 tbsp. finely chopped celery	dressing
1 tbsp. finely chopped	3 tbsp. milk
pimento	2 tsp. lemon juice
1/2 tsp. minced onion	1 tsp. prepared mustard
1/4 tsp. dry mustard	

Remove stems from mushrooms, cutting into mushrooms to form a cavity. Place the mushrooms, rounded side up, on a baking sheet and brush tops with 1/4 cup melted butter. Broil 3 to 4 inches from heat for 2 to 3 minutes or until lightly browned. Remove from broiler. Combine the bread crumbs, 3 tablespoons melted butter, celery, pimento, onion and dry mustard. Drain and flake the crab meat, then remove cartilage. Add to crumb mixture and mix well. Fill cavity of each mushroom with crab mixture. Combine the sour cream, mayonnaise, milk, lemon juice and prepared mustard in blazer pan of chafing dish. Place over water pan. Cook and stir until hot. Arrange filled mushrooms, rounded side down, in sauce and heat through.

Mrs. O. L. Parke, Saint Petersburg, Florida

STUFFED CUCUMBER RINGS
Prepare ahead; chill until serving time

2 med. cucumbers	1 1/2 tsp. Worcestershire
2 3-oz. packages cream	sauce
cheese	1/8 tsp. garlic powder
1/2 tsp. seasoned salt	Paprika
1/4 tsp. onion salt	Chopped parsley
1 tbsp. lemon juice	

Peel the cucumbers and remove centers with apple corer. Soften the cream cheese in a bowl. Add remaining ingredients except paprika and parsley and mix well. Stuff cavities of cucumbers with cream cheese mixture and chill until firm. Slice thin and sprinkle with paprika and parsley.

Mrs. H. A. Bowen, Jackson, Tennessee

THE OLIVER
Prepare ahead; ready to cut and serve

1 lge. round loaf French	1 lge. green pepper, cut
bread, split	in rings
Soft butter	2 c. well-drained pitted
12 thin slices mild cheese	California ripe olives
18 slices dry salami	

Hollow out a portion of the soft crumbs from both halves and spread the bread with soft butter. Cover the bottom half with the cheese, salami, green pepper and olives and top with remaining half of the bread loaf. Wrap in waxed paper to crush the olives and blend the flavors. Cut into 6 or 8 wedges.

Photograph for this recipe on page 14.

Angostura Smoky Frank Bites (below)

ANGOSTURA SMOKY FRANK BITES
Prepare ahead; 5 minutes cooking time

1 lb. skinless frankfurters	1/4 tsp. onion salt
2 tbsp. butter or margarine	1/4 tsp. garlic salt
1 1/2 tsp. angostura aromatic	1/4 tsp. celery salt
bitters	

Cut the frankfurters into 1-inch pieces. Heat the butter in a skillet and stir in remaining ingredients. Add the frankfurter pieces and stir until coated. Cook over medium heat, stirring occasionally, until the pieces are dark brown and crusty. Spear on toothpicks and serve hot.

HAM AND CHICKEN IN CRANBERRY SAUCE
Partially prepared ahead; keep warm for serving

1 c. sugar	1 tbsp. lemon juice
1/2 lb. fresh cranberries	Fully cooked ham and
1/4 c. catsup	chicken, cubed

Combine the sugar and 1 cup water in a saucepan and stir until sugar is dissolved. Heat to boiling point and boil for 5 minutes. Add the cranberries and cook for about 5 minutes or until skins pop. Remove from heat. Stir in the catsup and lemon juice. Pour into small blazer pan and place the ham and chicken cubes in sauce. Keep warm over hot water. Spear with cocktail picks to serve.

Mrs. W. M. Foster, Princeton, West Virginia

Kraut-Corned Beef Toasted Sandwich (below)

KRAUT-CORNED BEEF TOASTED SANDWICH
Preparation and cooking time less than 30 minutes

1 8-oz. can sauerkraut, well-drained	Salt
1/4 c. chopped green pepper	12 slices rye bread
1/4 c. chopped onion	6 slices Swiss cheese
1/4 c. creamy Russian dressing	6 slices corned beef
1/4 tsp. coarsely ground black pepper	2 eggs
	1/3 c. milk
	1/2 vegetable shortening

Combine the sauerkraut, green pepper, onion, dressing and pepper and mix well, then season with salt to taste. Top 6 bread slices with cheese, corned beef and the sauerkraut mixture and cover with remaining bread. Beat eggs, milk and 1/4 teaspoon salt together in a 9-inch pie plate or shallow dish. Heat the shortening in a large, heavy skillet. Dip each sandwich in the egg mixture, coating both sides. Brown on both sides in the hot shortening over medium heat. Serve immediately.

HOT DEVILED HAM SANDWICH
Easily prepared in 15 minutes

1 4 1/2-oz. can deviled ham	Cheese slices
1/4 c. pickle relish	6 tomato slices
12 slices white bread	Margarine, melted
Salad dressing	

Mix the ham and pickle relish well. Spread the bread with the salad dressing. Cover half the bread slices with cheese, ham mixture and tomatoes. Top the tomatoes with a second slice of cheese. Cover with remaining bread. Brush with margarine and grill on both sides until lightly browned. 6 servings.

Mrs. Craig Miller, Boise City, Oklahoma

HAWAIIAN SANDWICHES
Quick leftovers dividend; 15 minutes to assemble

1 c. minced cooked chicken	1/2 tsp. lemon juice
1/2 c. shredded coconut	1/2 tsp. salt
1/4 c. salad dressing	6 frankfurter buns
2 tbsp. chopped celery	

Combine the first 6 ingredients, blending well. Cut the frankfurter buns in half and spread the chicken mixture between the halves of the buns. 6 servings.

Mrs. L. E. Lennox, Brownsville, Texas

HAM-CHEESE CRUNCH SANDWICH
Easily prepared; 15 minutes to cook

8 slices white bread	1 tomato, thinly sliced
Softened margarine	2 eggs, slightly beaten
Prepared mustard	2 tbsp. milk
4 slices boiled ham	Dash of onion salt
4 slices process American cheese	1 1/4 c. crushed potato chips

Spread the bread on one side with margarine and mustard. Top 4 slices bread with the ham, cheese and tomato slices and cover with remaining bread. Combine the eggs, milk and onion salt. Dip the sandwiches in the egg mixture, then coat with the potato chips, patting to secure the chips to bread. Brown on both sides in a buttered skillet or griddle till crisp. Serve hot. 4 servings.

Mrs. F. F. Evans, McAlester, Oklahoma

QUICK VISITOR'S LUNCHEON
Potage de Garbanzos *page 40*
Easy Tomato Aspic *page 36*
Little Corned Beef Sandwich *page 25*

LITTLE CORNED BEEF SANDWICH
Emergency shelf ingredients; mix and cook for 10 minutes

4 English muffins	1 can corned beef hash
Butter	1 sm. can tomato sauce
4 slices American cheese	2 tsp. Worcestershire sauce

Split and butter the English muffins. Cut the cheese slices in half diagonally. Mix the hash, tomato sauce and Worcestershire sauce and spoon onto the muffins. Broil for about 5 minutes. Top with the cheese and broil until cheese begins to melt. Serve warm. 8 servings.

Mrs. Helen F. Reed, San Antonio, Texas

Monte Cristo Sandwich (below)

MONTE CRISTO SANDWICH
Easily prepared; 15 minutes cooking time

1/3 c. soft butter	**8 slices Swiss cheese**
1/2 tsp. curry powder	**1/4 lb. sliced cooked**
1/4 c. salad dressing	**chicken**
8 slices day-old white bread	

Combine the butter and curry powder and mix well. Spread 1/2 tablespoon salad dressing evenly over one side of the 8 bread slices. Top each of 4 slices of bread with a cheese slice, 1/4 of the chicken and a second cheese slice. Cover with remaining bread slices, salad dressing side down, then press sandwiches together firmly. Spread bread on both sides of each sandwich with an equal amount of curry butter. Brown sandwiches on both sides on a moderately hot grill or in frypan over moderate heat, turning sandwiches until golden brown on both sides. Serve immediately. 4 sandwiches or servings.

HAMBURGER CLUB SANDWICHES
Prepared and cooked in 15 minutes

1 lb. ground beef	**8 thin slices tomato**
12 slices white sandwich	**12 slices bacon, cooked crisp**
bread, toasted	**1 1/3 c. (about) sweet fresh**
Mayonnaise	**cucumber pickles**
Shredded lettuce	

Shape the ground beef into 4 square thin hamburgers 1/2-inch larger than slice of bread. Make hamburger 4 x 4 x 1/2 inches, if bread measures 3 1/2 x 4 inches. Broil 3 to 4 inches from source of heat for 4 to 5 minutes on each side or to desired doneness. Make each sandwich with a slice of toast spread with mayonnaise, a layer of lettuce, tomato and bacon slices, a second slice of toast, pickles, hamburger and a third slice of toast. Cut each sandwich in half diagonally and garnish with additional pickle slices on wooden picks.

HOMEMADE BARBECUED PORK
Quick leftovers dividend; 30 minutes cooking time

3 c. chopped roast pork	1/2 c. mustard
1 c. catsup	2 med. onions, chopped
1 c. water	1/2 tsp. pepper
1/2 tsp. salt	Buns
1/4 tsp. paprika	

Combine all the ingredients except the buns in a heavy skillet and simmer for 30 minutes or until thickened. Serve over the buns. 12 servings.

Mrs. Clayton Emmett, Jackson, Kentucky

TOMATO WIGGLE SANDWICH
Quickly prepared; 15 minutes cooking time

1 lb. sliced bacon	Mayonnaise
4 lge. tomatoes	6 slices American cheese
12 slices bread	

Fry the bacon until crisp and drain on paper towels. Peel and slice the tomatoes. Spread one side of each bread slice with mayonnaise. Place the cheese on 6 slices and top with tomato slices. Place 2 slices of bacon over the tomatoes and top with remaining bread slices. Lettuce leaves may be added, if desired.

Mrs. Stephen Riley, Anniston, Alabama

Hamburger Club Sandwiches (page 26)

Pineapple Fruit Mold Salad (page 30)

salads
& soups

Salads and soups are two kinds of dishes homemakers in a hurry know they can depend on for family approval and timesaving preparation. Consider, too, how versatile these two are: salads and soups can be served hot or cold . . . as a first course . . . a main dish . . . or even as a snack. With so much in their favor, it's no wonder that salads and soups have been relied upon to create a meal in minutes by generations of southern homemakers.

These women perfected their families' favorite recipes for salads and soups, and now the finest of these recipes — chosen especially for their short length of preparation — are included in this section's pages. Just imagine how much your hungry family and guests will enjoy the flavor contrast and brilliant color of a Cranberry-Raspberry Salad — or win compliments for yourself by featuring Marquise Chicken Salad.

The soups highlighted in this section are just as exciting. Serve your family Ground Beef-Vegetable Soup . . . Chicken Velvet Soup, as elegant and smooth as its name implies . . . Quick Crab Bisque, an updated version of an old southern favorite .

You can serve these marvelous salads and soups with confidence, knowing that they are the home-tested favorites of the women who proudly sign them. In fact, why not begin to earn warm compliments for yourself by serving one of these dishes tonight!

PINEAPPLE FRUIT MOLD SALAD
Prepare ahead; chill until serving time

1 8 1/2-oz. can pineapple tidbits	1/4 c. orange juice
1 3-oz. package strawberry gelatin	1 sliced banana
	1/2 c. melon balls or cubes
	1/4 c. sliced strawberries

Drain the pineapple, reserving the syrup. Measure the reserved syrup, adding enough water to make 1 cup liquid. Heat to boiling point and add the gelatin, stirring until dissolved, then remove from heat. Add 1/2 cup water and the orange juice and chill until slightly thickened. Fold in the pineapple, banana, melon and strawberries and turn into a 3-cup mold. Chill until firm, then unmold. Garnish with additional pineapple tidbits, if desired. Serve with mayonnaise or sour cream. 5 or 6 servings.

Photograph for this recipe on page 28.

MELBA PEACH SALAD
Allow 1 hour for softening cream cheese; assemble at serving time

1 No. 303 can peach halves	Lettuce leaves
1 3-oz. package cream cheese	Paprika
Mayonnaise	

Drain the peaches and reserve 1/2 cup syrup. Soften the cream cheese at room temperature. Mix the cream cheese, reserved syrup and enough mayonnaise to blend well with a fork. Arrange the lettuce leaves on a serving platter and place the peaches on the lettuce. Fill the peach halves with the cream cheese mixture and sprinkle with paprika. 6 servings.

Photograph for this recipe on page 2.

CHRYSANTHEMUM SALAD
Prepare ahead; chill until serving time

4 sm. grapefruit	4 med. oranges, cut up
3 med. red apples	1 c. walnut halves
1 8 1/2-oz. can apricot halves	

Make 6 equally spaced cuts through the grapefruit peel from the top to within 1 inch of the base using a sharp knife. Pull each piece of peel away from fruit, forming six petals attached at the base. Remove fruit carefully from the base, then remove the white membrane from grapefruit. Cut the grapefruit into sections, removing seeds and set aside. Cut each section of grapefruit peel into several narrow strips. Cut the apples into large pieces and add to the grapefruit sections. Drain the apricots and add, with the oranges to the grapefruit mixture. Add the walnuts and toss lightly. Refrigerate until ready to serve. Fill the grapefruit shells with the fruit mixture and place on lettuce leaves. Serve with favorite fruit salad dressing. 4 servings.

Margaret Kittlitz, Waco, Texas

CRANBERRY-RASPBERRY SALAD
Prepare ahead; chill until serving time

2 pkg. raspberry gelatin	1 pkg. frozen raspberries
1 can whole cranberries	1 c. sour cream

Prepare the gelatin according to package directions and cool slightly. Add the cranberries and raspberries. Pour half the mixture in a shallow dish. Chill until firm and smooth sour cream over the top. Pour the remaining gelatin mixture over the sour cream and chill until firm. 12 servings.

Mrs. Margaret Roberson, Ft. Lauderdale, Florida

SPICED WALNUT FRUIT SALAD
Preparation and cooking time less than 30 minutes

2 tsp. butter	1/2 c. fresh cranberries
2/3 c. California walnut halves	1 c. red grapes
and pieces	4 c. torn crisp lettuce
1 tbsp. sugar	1 c. mayonnaise
1/2 tsp. cinnamon	2 tbsp. orange juice
1 lge. red apple	1/4 tsp. grated orange peel

Melt the butter in a skillet. Add the walnuts and sprinkle with the sugar and cinnamon. Stir over moderate heat for about 5 minutes or until walnuts are lightly toasted, then cool. Core and cut the apple in small wedges. Halve the cranberries and remove the grape seeds. Turn the lettuce into a chilled salad bowl. Arrange the walnuts and fruits on top. Serve with mayonnaise blended with orange juice and peel. 6 servings.

Spiced Walnut Fruit Salad (above)

MARQUISE CHICKEN SALAD
Quick leftovers dividend; prepare in 20 minutes

3 c. cooked diced chicken	2 med. pickles, chopped
1 c. diced celery	Juice of 1/2 lemon
3 hard-cooked eggs, chopped	Salt and pepper to taste
1 lge. pimento, chopped	Salad dressing to taste
1/2 c. chopped pecans	

Combine all the ingredients and serve on crisp lettuce. 6 servings.

Myrtle P. Teer, Hutto, Texas

RUSH HOUR LUNCH

Tuna Spring Salad *page 32*
Cheese Biscuits *page 174*
Raspberry Chiffon Pie *page 169*

TUNA SPRING SALAD
Prepare in 20 minutes; serve immediately

2 c. cottage cheese	1 c. chopped parsley
1/2 tsp. Worcestershire sauce	2 tbsp. dietetic pickle relish
2 7-oz. cans dietetic tuna	Salt and pepper to taste
1 c. shredded carrot	

Mix the cottage cheese and Worcestershire sauce. Drain the tuna and break into flakes with a fork. Mix the tuna, vegetables and cottage cheese mixture. Toss lightly, then season with salt and pepper. Serve on lettuce and garnish with tomato wedges. 6 servings.

Mrs. Mary Lyons, Tuscaloosa, Alabama

CAESAR SALAD
Elegant but quickly prepared; 5 minutes for cooking croutons

Salad oil	1/4 tsp. pepper
2 cloves of garlic	3 qt. shredded salad greens
2 c. bread cubes	1/3 c. Parmesan cheese
3 tbsp. vinegar	1/3 c. crumbled blue cheese
1 tsp. Worcestershire sauce	6 anchovy fillets
1/2 tsp. salt	1 egg

Combine 1/4 cup salad oil with a split garlic clove in a skillet. Add the bread cubes and fry until crisp and golden brown. Mash the remaining garlic and add 1/3 cup salad oil, vinegar, Worcestershire sauce, salt and pepper. Place the salad greens in a wooden bowl and top with cheeses and anchovies. Strain the garlic from the dressing, then pour the dressing over salad. Break the egg over the salad and toss until egg is not visible. Add the croutons and toss lightly. Serve immediately. 6-8 servings.

Mrs. M. D. Lope, Wichita Falls, Texas

MOLDED TUNA-TOMATO SALAD
Partially prepared ahead; assemble at serving time

1 env. unflavored gelatin	1 7-oz. can tuna, drained
3/4 c. chili sauce	1/2 c. finely chopped celery
2 c. cottage cheese	1/4 c. sliced green onions
1 c. sour cream	Hard-cooked eggs, cut in
1/2 tsp. prepared mustard	wedges
1/2 tsp. sugar	Tomato wedges
1/4 tsp. salt	Green pepper strips

Soften the gelatin in 1/4 cup cold water. Bring the chili sauce to a boil in a small saucepan. Add the softened gelatin and stir until dissolved, then set aside. Combine the cottage cheese, sour cream, mustard, sugar and salt in a large bowl and stir until blended. Fold in the tuna, celery, onions and chili sauce mixture. Pour into a 6-cup mold and chill until firm. Unmold onto a chilled plate and surround with the eggs, tomatoes and green pepper. Serve with Lemon Sour Cream Dressing. 8 servings.

Lemon Sour Cream Dressing

1 tbsp. lemon juice	1/4 tsp. salt
1/2 tsp. sugar	1 c. sour cream

Blend the lemon juice, sugar and salt together in a small bowl and fold in the sour cream.

Molded Tuna-Tomato Salad (above)

Hot Sauced Potato Salad (below)

HOT SAUCED POTATO SALAD
Easily prepared; allow 2 to 3 hours to chill

3 lb. potatoes	1 c. mayonnaise
1 sm. onion, chopped	2 tbsp. prepared mustard
2 c. diced celery	2 tbsp. vinegar
2 tsp. salt	1/2 tsp. hot sauce

Cook the potatoes in skins until tender, then peel and dice. Add the onion and celery and sprinkle with salt. Mix mayonnaise, mustard, vinegar and hot sauce together and add to the potato mixture. Mix lightly with a fork being careful not to break potatoes and chill. Garnish with cucumbers, if desired. 12 servings.

ASPARAGUS VINAIGRETTE
Allow several hours for marinating, then ready to serve

1 can asparagus spears	6 tbsp. wine vinegar
1 sm. bottle olive oil	1 tsp. dry mustard
1 tsp. salt	1 tbsp. chopped capers
1/4 tsp. paprika	1 tbsp. chopped parsley
1 clove of garlic	1 tbsp. chopped chives

Drain the asparagus. Combine remaining ingredients and pour over the asparagus. Marinate for several hours. 6 servings.

Mrs. Leona Danielson, Baton Rouge, Louisiana

GOURMET TOSSED GREEN SALAD
Prepare ahead; add dressing at serving time

1 med. head lettuce	1 sm. sweet onion
1 sm. cauliflower	1 med. green pepper, diced

1 pimento, diced	1/2 c. Roquefort cheese
6 lge. fresh mushrooms, sliced	Low-calorie French dressing

Tear the lettuce into bite-sized pieces. Separate the cauliflower into tiny flowerets. Cut the onion in paper-thin rings. Toss the flowerets and onion rings gently with green pepper, pimento, mushrooms and cheese. Chill for about 1 hour. Toss with French dressing and serve immediately.

Mrs. Marvin L. Lane, Nashville, Tennessee

COLESLAW WITH SOUR CREAM DRESSING
Prepare ahead; assemble at serving time

3 tbsp. (heaping) sour cream	3 tbsp. vinegar
3/4 c. sugar	1/2 c. milk
3/4 tsp. salt	3 c. shredded cabbage

Combine the sour cream, sugar and salt, stirring well. Add the vinegar and stir well. Stir in milk and correct seasonings, if necessary. Refrigerate for several minutes to thicken. Blend in the cabbage and serve. 5-7 servings.

Mrs. Sara Callahan, Jackson, Mississippi

MARINATED GREEN BEAN SALAD
May be prepared days ahead

2 9-oz. packages frozen French-style green beans	1 tsp. salt
3 tbsp. cider vinegar	Dash of pepper
1 1/2 tbsp. salad oil	1/2 tsp. chopped parsley

Cook the beans according to package directions and drain. Turn into a shallow serving dish and refrigerate for 1 hour or until well chilled. Combine remaining ingredients in a jar with a tight-fitting lid, then cover and shake vigorously. Pour over the beans and toss gently until well coated. Refrigerate until ready to serve, then toss lightly. 6 servings.

Mrs. Alan Hanna, Baton Rouge, Louisiana

MIXED VEGETABLE SALAD
Prepare ahead; chill until serving time

1 1-lb. 8-oz. package frozen mixed vegetables	1/4 c. chopped green pepper
1/4 c. chopped scallions, including tops	3/4 c. salad dressing
	Salt and pepper to taste

Cook the mixed vegetables according to package directions and drain. Add the scallions and green pepper and cool. Add the salad dressing, salt and pepper. Store in refrigerator until ready to use. Garnish with tomato wedges, if desired. 6-8 servings.

Mrs. Arthur Ingram, Laurel, Mississippi

PICKLED ONION AND BEET SLICES
Allow 8 hours for marinating, then ready to serve

2 tbsp. sugar	1 med. onion, sliced
1/4 c. vinegar	1 can sliced beets, drained
1/4 c. salad oil	Lettuce
Salt and pepper to taste	

Mix the sugar, vinegar, salad oil, salt and pepper. Place the onion and beet slices in a bowl and add the vinegar mixture. Refrigerate for 8 to 12 hours or overnight. Serve on lettuce.

Mrs. J. Mitchell Murry, Ft. Campbell, Kentucky

TOMATO SALAD
Partially prepared ahead; allow 20 minutes for final preparation

1 tbsp. salt	1 med. onion, chopped
1/2 c. sugar	1/2 c. catsup
1 1/2 tsp. pepper	1 c. salad oil
1 tsp. dry mustard	1 head lettuce, shredded
1/2 c. vinegar	4 tomatoes, cut in wedges

Combine all the ingredients except lettuce and tomatoes in a blender and blend until smooth. Arrange the lettuce on salad plates and place the tomato wedges on the lettuce. Serve with the dressing. The dressing may be blended and refrigerated, covered, for several hours.

Mrs. Rachel Hudson, Dublin, Georgia

EASY TOMATO ASPIC
Easily prepared in 15 minutes; allow several hours for congealing

2 sm. packages lemon gelatin	1 tsp. salt
1 8-oz. can tomato sauce	1 c. diced celery
2 tbsp. vinegar	10 sliced olives

Dissolve the gelatin in 2 1/2 cups boiling water, then add the tomato sauce. Add the vinegar, salt, celery and olives and pour into a large mold. Chill until firm.

Mrs. Edison F. Arnold, San Antonio, Texas

CONGEALED VEGETABLE SALAD
Prepare ahead; chill until serving time

1 pkg. orange gelatin	1 c. diced green onions
1/2 tsp. salt	1 c. diced celery
1 c. shredded carrots	

Dissolve the gelatin in 1 cup hot water then add the salt and 1 cup cold water. Chill until partially set, then fold in remaining ingredients. Pour into an oiled 1 1/2-quart mold and chill until firm. 6-8 servings.

Mrs. Dorothy M. Ham, Nahunta, Georgia

GROUND BEEF-VEGETABLE SOUP
Easily prepared in 15 minutes; allow 1 hour for cooking

1 lb. ground beef	1/4 tsp. pepper
2 c. frozen mixed vegetables	1 bay leaf
2 c. wide noodles	1 beef bouillon cube
1 tsp. salt	

Brown the ground beef in a skillet. Cook the mixed vegetables according to package directions. Combine the vegetables and liquid, noodles, ground beef, salt, pepper, bay leaf, bouillon cube and 6 cups water in a large pot. Simmer for 50 minutes, adding water if needed. Remove the bay leaf and serve.

Mrs. Judy Thomas, Alexander City, Alabama

CHICKEN VELVET SOUP
Quick leftovers dividend; 30 minutes cooking time

6 tbsp. butter or margarine	3 c. chicken broth
1/3 c. all-purpose flour	1 c. minced cooked chicken
1/2 c. milk	Dash of pepper
1/2 c. light cream	

Melt the butter in a saucepan and blend in the flour. Add the milk, cream and broth. Cook, stirring, until thickened. Stir in the chicken and pepper and cook until heated through. Garnish with chopped parsley and pimento cut into star shape, if desired. 4 servings.

Rachel L. Keisler, Marion, North Carolina

BLENDER OYSTER STEW
Prepared and ready to serve in 15 minutes

1 8-oz. can oysters	1/4 tsp. salt
3 tbsp. margarine	1 tsp. chili powder
2 c. milk	

Place the oysters and 1 cup water in a blender and chop for 2 seconds. Pour into a boiler and simmer for 2 to 3 minutes, stirring occasionally. Add margarine, milk and salt and heat but do not boil. Add the chili powder and stir. 4-6 servings.

Mrs. Roy Harwood, Taylor, Texas

QUICK CRAB BISQUE
Emergency shelf ingredients; mix and cook for 15 minutes

1 can green pea soup	1/2 tsp. paprika
1 can tomato soup	1 can crab meat, flaked
1 1/2 soup cans milk	1/4 c. sherry
1/4 tsp. curry powder	

Combine the soups, milk and seasonings in a saucepan. Heat, but do not boil. Stir in the crab meat and sherry. Reheat and serve. 4 servings.

Mrs. Ella Adams, Morgantown, West Virginia

Rock Lobster-Corn Soup Stew (below)

ROCK LOBSTER-CORN SOUP STEW
Elegant but quickly prepared; 30 minutes for cooking

2 8-oz. packages frozen South African rock lobster-tails	1/4 c. flour
	4 c. milk
1/4 c. butter or margarine	1 1-lb. can cream-style corn
1 sm. onion, minced	Salt to taste
1/2 c. chopped celery	Paprika to taste
1/2 c. chopped fresh mushrooms	Cayenne pepper to taste

Thaw the lobster-tails. Remove the underside membrane with scissors, then pull out meat in 1 piece and cut into crosswise slices. Melt the butter and saute the onion, celery and mushrooms until tender but not brown. Stir in the flour. Stir in the milk gradually. Cook over low heat, stirring constantly, until soup thickens slightly. Add the corn and rock lobster pieces. Season with salt, paprika and cayenne. Cook and stir over low heat until the rock lobster pieces are white and opaque. Sprinkle with paprika at serving time. 6-8 servings.

SHELTON'S SEAFOOD GUMBO
Prepare ahead; allow 30 minutes to reheat and serve

1 lb. chicken backs and necks	1 bunch celery, chopped
Cooking oil	1 lb. okra, chopped
2 c. flour	1 c. chopped parsley
1 lb. salt pork, chopped	1 bunch shallots, chopped

3 cloves of garlic, chopped
2 lge. green peppers, chopped
2 sm. cans tomato paste
1 qt. oysters

2 lb. shrimp, cleaned and
  deveined
1 can crab meat
1 tbsp. (about) gumbo file

Boil the chicken pieces in water to cover until well done. Cool and remove the meat from bones, reserving stock. Heat 1 cup oil to the boiling point and add the flour slowly, stirring constantly. Cook and stir until brown. Heat 1 tablespoon oil in a skillet, then add the salt pork and simmer for about 5 minutes. Place the vegetables, flour mixture and salt pork in a large cooking pot and thin with reserved stock, tomato paste and enough water to fill pot 3/4 full. Bring to a rolling boil, then reduce heat and simmer for 1 hour. Add the chicken meat, oysters, shrimp and crab meat and cook over low heat for 30 minutes, stirring occasionally. Add gumbo file and simmer for 10 minutes, stirring occasionally. Freeze in desired amounts.

Mrs. Shelton W. Watts, New Orleans, Louisiana

SHRIMP JAMBALAYA
Easily prepared; allow 1 hour for cooking

2 tsp. salt
1 tsp. hot sauce
1 bay leaf
1 stalk celery with leaves
1 lb. shrimp
1/4 c. butter
1/2 c. chopped onion

1/2 c. chopped green pepper
1 garlic clove, minced
1 c. rice
1 1-lb. can tomatoes
3/4 c. bouillon
1 1/2 c. diced cooked ham

Place 3 cups water, 1 teaspoon salt and 1/2 teaspoon hot sauce in a saucepan and add the bay leaf and celery. Bring to a boil and add the shrimp. Bring to a boil again and cook for 5 minutes. Drain the shrimp and cool quickly. Shell and devein the shrimp. Melt the butter in a large skillet, then add the onion, green pepper and garlic. Cook until the onion is tender, but not brown. Stir in the rice, tomatoes, bouillon, remaining salt and hot sauce. Bring to a boil over high heat, then reduce the temperature and cover the skillet. Simmer for 20 minutes. Add the ham, then cover and cook until the liquid is absorbed. 4-6 servings.

Photograph for this recipe on page 2.

PUMPKIN SOUP
Preparation and cooking time less than 1 hour

4 c. milk
1 c. cooked pumpkin
1/2 tsp. salt

1/4 tsp. cinnamon
1 tbsp. sugar
1/2 c. rice

Heat the milk in a large saucepan and add remaining ingredients. Cook over low heat for about 30 minutes or until rice is well done. Yield: 4 servings.

Mrs. Virginia T. Krueger, Richmond, Virginia

CABBAGE CHOWDER
Preparation and cooking time less than 1 hour

4 c. shredded cabbage	1/2 tsp. pepper
2 c. sliced carrots	1/2 tsp. sugar
3 c. diced potatoes	2 tbsp. butter
1 tbsp. salt	4 c. milk

Combine the vegetables, salt, pepper, sugar and 2 cups water in a large saucepan or Dutch oven and cook over low heat until the vegetables are done. Add the butter and milk. Serve hot with crackers. 8 servings.

Mrs. Homer E. Miller, Marietta, Georgia

POTAGE DE GARBANZOS
Partially prepared ahead; allow 1 hour for cooking

3/4 lb. garbanzos	1 onion, finely chopped
Salt	1/4 c. lard
1 beef bone	1/2 lb. potatoes, cubed
1 hambone	1 pinch of saffron
4 oz. white bacon	1 chorizo, sliced thin

Cover garbanzos with water and add 1 teaspoon salt. Soak overnight, then drain. Add the beef bone, hambone and 1 1/2 quarts water and cook for 45 minutes over low heat. Fry the bacon and onion in the lard until browned and add to the garbanzo mixture. Add water to cover. Add the potatoes, saffron and salt to taste and cook until potatoes are done. Remove from heat and add the chorizo. Chorizo is Spanish sausage. 4 servings.

Mrs. Herbert A. Schert, Jacksonville, Florida

COLD WEATHER SPECIAL
Vegetable Beef Soup *page 40*
Bubbly Cheese Toast *page 175*
Sherried Fruit Compote *page 166*

VEGETABLE BEEF SOUP
Easily prepared; allow 2 hours for cooking

1 lb. boneless stew beef	1 c. diced potatoes
1 pt. small lima beans	1/2 stick margarine
1 pt. whole-kernel corn	2 tbsp. salt
1 qt. cut-up tomatoes	1 tbsp. sugar
1 c. diced carrots	

Place the beef in 1/2 gallon water and boil for about 30 minutes. Add remaining ingredients; cook for about 1 hour and 30 minutes or until vegetables are tender.

Mrs. Orris E. Wood, Nashville, North Carolina

MARVELOUS JULY COOLER

Chilled Vichyssoise *page 41*
Hot Deviled Ham Sandwich *page 24*
Chocolate Candy Bar Icebox Pie *page 168*

CHILLED VICHYSSOISE
Prepare ahead; chill until serving time

4 or 5 leeks	3 c. milk
1/4 c. butter	1 tsp. salt
3 c. thinly sliced potatoes	1/8 tsp. white pepper
1 c. hot water	1/8 tsp. paprika
4 chicken bouillon cubes	1 c. cream

Slice the leeks thin, using only white and very light green portions to measure 1 1/2 cups. Melt the butter in a large, heavy saucepan. Add the leeks and cook and stir until transparent but not brown. Add the potatoes, water and bouillon cubes. Cover and cook over moderate heat until tender. Press through a fine sieve or puree in the blender, then return to the saucepan. Add the milk, stirring rapidly to blend. Stir in the salt, white pepper and paprika. Add the cream and heat only to blend flavors. Chill quickly and serve cold. 6 servings.

Mrs. Paul Lang, Leachville, Arkansas

TOMATO-CORN CHOWDER
Emergency shelf ingredients; mix and cook for 15 minutes

1 c. milk	1/2 c. cream-style corn
1 can tomato soup	1/4 tsp. curry powder

Add the milk gradually to the tomato soup. Stir in the corn. Sprinkle the curry powder on top and heat over low heat until very hot. 2-3 servings.

Mrs. John R. Harrison, Hopewell, Virginia

SPLIT PEA SOUP WITH HAM
Easily prepared in 15 minutes; allow 4 hours for cooking

1 meaty hambone	1 c. chopped celery
1 pkg. dry vegetable soup mix	3/4 lb. yellow or green split
2 med. onions, chopped	peas

Combine 2 quarts water with the hambone, soup mix and vegetables in a large kettle. Simmer for 4 hours, stirring occasionally. Add water if necessary. 8 servings.

Mrs. Joan Jurgelas, Roanoke, Virginia

COLORFUL SOUP AND SANDWICH MEAL

Split Pea Soup with Ham *page 41*
Tomato Wiggle Sandwich *page 27*
Brown Sugar Pudding *page 165*

Pennsylvania Dutch Burgers (page 56)

meats

The center of attraction at almost every meal is the meat dish — yet it is often this dish which presents the biggest problem for the homemaker in a hurry. Trying to create a quick and easy, flavor-filled, eye-appealing meat dish her family will enjoy is a problem which perplexes even the most innovative cook.

Southern homemakers have confronted this problem, and solved it with their usual creative flair, as the recipes in this section will reflect. Do you want to serve steak in an exciting, new, timesaving fashion? Then turn to the recipe for Teriyaki. It takes just minutes to prepare — in fact, you can cook it right at your table!

Earn even more compliments for yourself when you serve exotic South Seas Pot Roast . . . typically southern Saucy Short Ribs . . . Pork Chops in Rice . . . or any of the marvelous tried-and-proven recipes awaiting you in the pages that follow.

Even when you're planning a party, feature these recipes. Just imagine the oh's and ah's you'll be greeted by when you carry in Oven Shish Kabob . . . elegant Mushrooms with Lamb . . . or zesty Veal Parmesan. How perfect to serve such flavorful dishes — and how wonderful that such dishes take only a minimum of effort on your part.

When you want timesaving, compliment-drawing recipes for meats, this is the section you'll depend on!

Avocado Sirloin (below)

AVOCADO SIRLOIN
Elegant but quickly prepared; 20 minutes for cooking

1 2-in. sirloin steak	3 tbsp. horseradish
Salt and pepper to taste	1 tbsp. lemon juice
1/2 c. butter, melted	1 avocado, thinly sliced

Season the steak with salt and pepper and place on the broiler rack about 4 inches from the source of heat. Broil until brown on one side and turn. Broil until the second side begins to brown, then brush with the butter and sprinkle the horseradish and lemon juice on top. Place the avocado slices over the sauce and broil for 2 minutes longer. Garnish with parsley.

TERIYAKI
Allow 2 hours for marinating; prepared and cooked in 30 minutes

1/2 c. soy sauce	2 cloves of garlic, minced
1/4 c. sugar	Dash of pepper
1/4 tsp. ground ginger	2 to 3 lb. round steak
1/2 tsp. monosodium glutamate	

Mix first 6 ingredients and place in shallow dish. Add the steak and marinate for at least 2 hours in refrigerator. Place on a grill over hot coals and cook until brown on both sides. Thicken the marinade for gravy, if desired. Steak may be broiled in oven.

Mrs. Norman Doorenbos, University, Mississippi

BEEF WITH HORSERADISH
Elegant but quickly prepared; 20 minutes for cooking

4 cubed beef steaks
1 lge. onion, sliced
2 tbsp. butter or margarine
Salt and pepper to taste
2 tbsp. soy sauce

1/2 c. cooking sherry or broth
1 c. sour cream
2 tsp. prepared horseradish
2 tsp. chopped dill or dillseed

Brown the steaks and onion lightly in butter in a skillet. Add the salt, pepper, soy sauce and sherry and cover. Simmer for 20 minutes. Combine the sour cream, horseradish and dill and stir into the steak mixture. Heat through and serve on rice.

Mrs. A. J. Houdek, Sorrento, Florida

FRIDAY EVENING HOSTESS SPECIAL

Grilled T-bone Steak *page 45*
Caesar Salad *page 32*
Quick Breadsticks *page 175*
Strawberry Whip *page 158*

GRILLED T-BONE STEAK
Allow 2 to 3 hours for marinating; prepared and cooked in about 20 minutes

1 T-bone steak, 1 in. thick
1/4 c. wine vinegar
2 tbsp. salad oil
2 tbsp. soy sauce
2 tbsp. instant minced onion

1 tbsp. brown sugar
1/4 tsp. ground ginger
1/4 tsp. dry mustard
1/8 tsp. pepper
1 garlic clove, minced

Place the steak in a shallow bowl. Combine all remaining ingredients and pour over the steak. Cover and marinate in the refrigerator for 2 to 3 hours. Remove the steak from the marinade and slash edge at 2-inch intervals. Place on grill about 2 to 3 inches from coals. Broil steak for about 5 to 8 minutes on each side. 2-3 servings.

Mrs. L. B. Corbett, Augusta, Georgia

PANBROILED STEAK WITH BEAN SPROUTS
Preparation and cooking time less than 30 minutes

1 lge. sirloin steak, 1 1/2 in.
   thick
4 tbsp. butter

1 c. finely chopped green onions
2 c. bean sprouts
2 tbsp. soy sauce

Brown the steak on both sides in a small amount of fat in a heavy skillet. Place butter on steak and cook to desired doneness. Remove steak to a warm platter. Stir the green onions, bean sprouts and soy sauce into drippings in the skillet and cook until tender, stirring frequently. Serve with the steak. 6 servings.

Mrs. John D. Thompson, Fort Worth, Texas

EASY HAMBURGER-CARROT SKILLET DISH
Prepared and cooked in 1 hour

1 lb. ground beef	1/4 c. parsley flakes
1 pkg. onion soup mix	1 c. sliced carrots
4 1/2 c. boiling water	1 8-oz. package noodles
2 bouillon cubes	

Brown the ground beef in an electric skillet and drain. Add the onion soup mix, boiling water, bouillon cubes, parsley and sliced carrots and simmer for 15 minutes. Add the noodles, then cover and simmer until tender. 4 servings.

Mrs. Minnie Corley, Bluefield, West Virginia

GROUND BEEF IN SOUR CREAM
Elegant but quickly prepared; 40 minutes for cooking

1 lb. ground beef	Dash of pepper
1 c. chopped onion	2 tsp. Worcestershire sauce
3 c. med. noodles	1/4 c. chopped green pepper
3 c. tomato juice	1 c. sour cream
1 tsp. salt	1 3-oz. can sliced mushrooms
1 1/2 tsp. celery salt	

Brown the ground beef lightly in a large skillet. Add the chopped onion and cook until tender, but not brown. Place the noodles in a layer over the ground beef. Combine tomato juice, salt, celery salt, pepper and Worcestershire sauce and pour over the noodles. Bring to a boil, then cover and simmer over low heat for 20 minutes. Add the green pepper and cover. Cook for 10 minutes or until the noodles are tender. Stir in the sour cream and mushrooms. Heat just to boiling point. Season to taste. 6 servings.

Andrea Fletcher, Mountain Pine, Arkansas

HODGEPODGE
Emergency shelf ingredients; mix and cook for 30 minutes

1 lb. ground beef	1 can vegetable soup
2 tbsp. flour	1 can mushroom soup
Salt and pepper to taste	1/2 soup can milk

Brown the ground beef and sprinkle with the flour, salt and pepper. Add the soups and milk. Cook over medium heat for at least 30 minutes. Serve over Chinese noodles, toast or mashed potatoes. 4 servings.

Mrs. Eileen Patrick, Walnut Ridge, Arkansas

QUICKIE BEEF MEAL
Emergency shelf ingredients; mix and cook for 40 minutes

1 lb. ground chuck	4 tbsp. catsup
1 tbsp. fat	2 tbsp. water
1 sm. onion, chopped	1 No. 303 can macaroni with
1 tsp. salt	cheese sauce
1/2 tsp. pepper	

Combine the ground chuck, fat, onion, salt, pepper, catsup and water in a skillet and cook over medium heat for 30 minutes, stirring occasionally. Add the macaroni and cook over low heat for 10 minutes. Serve warm. 6 servings.

Mrs. Johnnie Walker, Hillsboro, Texas

MOCK FILET MIGNON
20 minutes to prepare; 20 minutes to cook

1 lb. ground chuck	1/4 tsp. pepper
1 tsp. salt	4 slices bacon

Combine the ground chuck with the salt and pepper and shape into 4 patties. Wrap each patty in bacon and secure with toothpicks. Broil on one side, then turn and broil on the other side. Serve hot. 4 servings.

Emmy Curlee, Portsmouth, Virginia

TWENTY-MINUTE MEAT LOAF
20 minutes to prepare; 20 minutes to bake

1 1/2 lb. ground beef	1 lge. egg
1/2 tsp. salt	1 c. soft bread crumbs
1/8 to 1/4 tsp. pepper	1 8-oz. can tomato sauce
2 tbsp. instant onion	

Combine all the ingredients as for meat loaf, then shape into 8 oval loaves. Place in shallow baking dish. Bake at 450 degrees for 15 minutes. Spoon off excess grease.

Sauce

1 8-oz. can tomato sauce	2 tbsp. parsley flakes
2 tbsp. brown sugar	1 tsp. Worcestershire sauce

Combine all the ingredients and pour over meat loaves. Bake for 5 minutes longer. 4 servings.

Mrs. Lucille Weaver, Gulfport, Mississippi

BROILED HAMBURGER PATTIES
Preparation and cooking time less than 1 hour

1 lb. hamburger	
Instant meat tenderizer	Worcestershire sauce
Pepper to taste	1 can tomato soup

Shape the hamburger into 4 large patties. Sprinkle both sides with tenderizer and season with pepper. Place in the broiler pan and brown on one side. Turn patties and sprinkle with Worcestershire sauce. Broil until brown. Dilute the tomato soup with a small amount of water and add 2 teaspoons Worcestershire sauce to season. Heat and serve over the hamburger patties. 4 servings.

Mrs. Becky Cole, Decatur, Georgia

BEEF TENDERLOIN WITH MUSHROOM STUFFING
Elegant but quickly prepared; 1 hour for baking

1 4-lb. beef tenderloin	1 1/2 c. soft bread crumbs
1/2 sm. onion, chopped	1/2 c. diced celery
1 4-oz. can mushrooms	Salt and pepper to taste
1/4 c. butter	4 slices bacon

Have tenderloin split and flattened at the market. Brown the onion and mushrooms in the butter in a heavy frypan. Add the bread crumbs, celery and enough hot water to moisten. Season with salt and pepper. Place the beef in a roasting pan and spread the stuffing over half the beef. Bring remaining half of the beef over stuffing and sew or skewer edges together. Season the beef and place bacon slices over top. Roast in 350-degree oven for 1 hour. 6-8 servings.

Maj. Carl S. Satterlund, Mobile, Alabama

KING'S ROAST
Easily prepared; allow 2 hours for cooking

1 6-lb. rump roast	Salt and pepper to taste
3 cloves of garlic	1 c. cold water
2 c. sifted flour	

Cut small slits all over the roast with sharp point of a knife. Cut garlic cloves lengthwise into slices. Place 1 slice in each slit. Combine flour, salt and pepper and coat the roast heavily. Place in roaster and sprinkle any leftover flour mixture on the bottom of the roaster. Pour the water into the roaster and cover. Roast in 450-degree oven for 2 hours for a well-done roast.

Mrs. W. P. Yoakum, McAllen, Texas

SOUTH SEAS POT ROAST
Easily prepared in 15 minutes; allow 4 hours to bake

1 4-lb. pot roast	1/2 c. soy sauce
2 tbsp. sugar	1 can tomato soup
1 tsp. ground ginger	4 med. onions

Place the roast in a deep baking pan. Mix the sugar, ginger, soy sauce and soup and pour over the roast. Cut the onions in thick slices and place over roast. Cover tightly. Bake at 300 degrees for about 4 hours. 6 servings.

Mrs. J. C. Taylor, Waynesboro, Mississippi

EASY ROAST BEEF AND GRAVY
Easily prepared; allow 2 to 4 hours for baking

1 3 to 5-lb. beef roast	1 can cream of mushroom soup
1 env. dry onion soup mix	

Place the roast in a large piece of heavy aluminum foil. Empty the soup mix over the roast, then add mushroom soup. Seal the foil and place on a shallow baking pan. Bake at 300 degrees for about 45 minutes per pound. 8 servings.

Mrs. Mary Menking, Gonzales, Texas

Easy Beef Roast Dinner (below)

EASY BEEF ROAST DINNER
Easily prepared; allow 2 hours for cooking

6 med. carrots, scraped	1 4-lb. pot roast
1 bay leaf	Salt and pepper to taste
1 tsp. parsley flakes	6 sm. onions, peeled
1/3 c. water	6 sm. potatoes, peeled

Season the roast with salt and pepper, then place in a plastic baking bag. Add the remaining ingredients and close the bag, then punch holes according to package directions. Bake at 350 degrees for about 2 hours or until the roast is tender. Arrange the vegetables around the roast on a serving platter. Discard the bay leaf.

CRANBERRY BEEF ROAST
Easily prepared; allow 3 hours for cooking

1 3 to 4-lb. rolled chuck roast	2 tbsp. fat
	Salt and pepper to taste
2 tbsp. flour	2 c. tart cranberry sauce

Dredge the roast with flour and brown well in hot fat in a roasting pan or Dutch oven. Season the roast with salt and pepper and cover with the cranberry sauce. Add 1 cup hot water and cover. Cook over low heat for about 3 hours or until tender. Add water, if necessary, to retain liquid in bottom of roasting pan. Remove the roast to a serving dish and thicken the pan liquid for gravy. 6-8 servings.

Mrs. Ross Gutierrez, Hurst, Texas

BARBECUED RIBS
Prepared and cooked in 1 hour

2 lb. beef ribs	1/2 tsp. dry mustard
2 tsp. fat	1 tsp. chili powder
1 onion, sliced	2 tbsp. vinegar
3 tbsp. brown sugar	1 pt. tomato juice
1 tsp. paprika	Salt and pepper to taste

Brown the ribs in fat in a heavy frypan and add remaining ingredients. Cover and cook over low heat for 45 minutes or until tender.

Mrs. S. H. Manuel, Wellington, Texas

SAUCY SHORT RIBS
Easily prepared; allow 1 hour and 30 minutes for cooking

2 lb. lean beef short ribs	1 1/2 tsp. salt
1/4 c. oil	1/8 tsp. pepper
1/2 c. chopped onion	2 8-oz. cans tomato sauce
1 tbsp. prepared horseradish	

Cut the beef ribs into 4 pieces and brown in hot oil in a skillet. Pour off excess oil. Combine remaining ingredients and pour over ribs. Cover and simmer for 1 hour and 30 minutes or until beef is tender, adding water, if needed. 4 servings.

Loretta Pennington, Cabins, West Virginia

EASY-ON-THE-HOSTESS COMPANY MENU

Oven Shish Kabobs *page 50*
Gourmet Tossed Green Salad *page 34*
Onion Bread *page 179*
Frozen Lemon Mousse *page 161*

OVEN SHISH KABOBS
Allow 2 hours for marinating; prepared and cooked in 30 minutes

1/2 lb. round steak, cut into squares	4 sm. white onions
1/2 c. water	2 green peppers
1/2 c. spicy French dressing	4 sm. tomatoes
1 tsp. salt	8 lge. mushrooms
1 tsp. pepper	8 sm. red potatoes

Marinate the steak in water and dressing for 2 hours or longer. Sprinkle with salt and pepper. Arrange the steak, onions, peppers, tomatoes, mushrooms and potatoes on long skewers. Set the skewers about 6 inches from source of heat and turn occasionally to allow even broiling. Broil for 25 minutes. 4 servings.

Mrs. R. R. Hill, Spartanburg, South Carolina

CREAMED BEEF WAFFLES WITH ALMONDS
20 minutes to prepare; 20 minutes to cook

1/2 c. sliced celery	4 c. milk
1 1/2 oz. dried beef	Dash of Worcestershire sauce
4 tbsp. butter	Waffles
4 tbsp. flour	Toasted almonds, slivered

Cook the celery in small amount of water in a saucepan until tender and drain. Cook the dried beef in the butter in a saucepan until frizzled, then stir in the flour. Add the milk slowly and cook, stirring constantly, until thickened. Season with Worcestershire sauce and stir in the celery. Serve on hot waffles and top with almonds. 8 servings.

Mrs. Preston Griffin, Pensacola, Florida

BEEF A LA STROGANOFF
Preparation and cooking time about 30 minutes

1 1-lb. flank steak	2 tbsp. tomato puree
1 1/2 tbsp. margarine	2 c. yogurt
1 lge. yellow onion	1 1/2 c. water
1/2 tsp. salt	Juice of 1/2 lemon
1/4 tsp. pepper	

Cut the steaks in thin strips about 2 inches long. Melt the margarine in a large frypan and brown the meat strips quickly. Lower the temperature and add the onion. Fry with the steak strips until the onion is clear. Season with salt and pepper. Add the tomato puree, yogurt, water and lemon juice. Cover and simmer for 10 to 15 minutes. Serve with boiled rice or boiled potatoes and a green salad.

Beef a la Stroganoff (above)

CHINESE GINGERED BEEF
20 minutes to prepare; 20 minutes to cook

1 lb. beef	4 tsp. sugar
1/2 c. fresh ginger	1/4 tsp. garlic powder
6 tbsp. oil	2 tbsp. cornstarch
6 tbsp. soy sauce	3/4 c. water
4 tsp. sauterne or sherry	

Cut the beef across the grain into thin slices. Slice the ginger 1/8 inch thick and place in oil in a skillet. Cook over moderately high heat until lightly browned. Add the beef slices and cook, stirring, until browned. Blend in soy sauce, sauterne, sugar and garlic powder and cook over high heat until liquid is absorbed. Mix the cornstarch with water and stir into the beef mixture. Cook for several minutes or until thickened. 4 servings.

Fonville Winans, Baton Rouge, Louisiana

EASY BUFFET SUPPER

Beef Stroganoff over Rice *page 52*
Asparagus Vinaigrette *page 34*
Herbed French Bread *page 178*
Crunchy Peaches and Cream *page 162*

BEEF STROGANOFF OVER RICE
Prepared and cooked in 1 hour

1 lb. round steak, cut into thin strips	1/4 c. water
1/2 c. chopped onion	1/2 c. sour cream
Garlic to taste	1/2 tsp. paprika
2 tbsp. butter or margarine	Salt and pepper to taste
1 can cream of mushroom soup	2 c. cooked rice

Brown the steak, onion and garlic in the butter, then remove the garlic. Stir in the soup, water, sour cream, paprika, salt and pepper and cover. Cook over low heat for 45 minutes or until the steak is tender, stirring frequently. Serve over rice. 4 servings.

Mrs. John K. Welch, Montgomery, Alabama

PEPPER STEAK CHOP SUEY
Preparation and cooking time less than 1 hour

2 lb. round steak	1 bunch celery, chopped
1/4 c. oil	1 c. chopped green peppers
1 tsp. garlic salt	1 can Chinese vegetables
1 c. diced onions	3/4 c. water
3 tbsp. soya sauce	2 tbsp. cornstarch
1 tbsp. molasses	

Cut the steak into small cubes and fry in oil in a skillet until brown. Add the garlic salt, onions, soya sauce, molasses, celery, green peppers and Chinese vegetables and bring to a boil. Mix the water with cornstarch and stir into steak mixture. Reduce heat and simmer until steak is tender.

Pearl H. Wright, Hollywood, Florida

FRENCH-FRIED LIVER STRIPS
Allow 30 minutes for marinating; prepared and cooked in 10 minutes

1 lb. liver	Seasoned flour
French dressing	

Cut the liver into 3 x 1/2-inch strips and marinate in French dressing for 30 minutes. Coat liver with seasoned flour. Fry in deep, hot fat for 5 minutes or until brown.

Mrs. Ernest Robinson, Sweetwater, Oklahoma

TANGERINE-GLAZED FRANKFURTERS
20 minutes to prepare; 20 minutes to cook

1 6-oz. can concentrated tangerine juice	1/3 tsp. dry mustard
4 tsp. cornstarch	1 tbsp. Worcestershire sauce
1/3 c. (firmly packed) light brown sugar	1/3 c. pickle relish
	2 lb. frankfurters

Mix the tangerine juice with 1 can water. Mix the cornstarch and sugar in a skillet, then add the tangerine juice. Add the remaining ingredients except the frankfurters and cook over low heat for 5 to 10 minutes or until thick, stirring frequently. Add the frankfurters and cook for 10 minutes longer or until frankfurters are glazed.

Martha Tate, Stigler, Oklahoma

SAUCY FRANK DINNER
Preparation and cooking time less than 1 hour

1 lb. frankfurters	1/2 c. water
1/2 c. chopped onion	1 tbsp. Worcestershire sauce
1 tbsp. butter or margarine	1 tsp. sugar
1 can tomato soup	Dash of hot sauce
1 8-oz. can tomato sauce	1/2 lb. bow tie noodles

Cut the frankfurters into quarters lengthwise. Saute the onion in butter until tender, then stir in the tomato soup, tomato sauce, water, Worcestershire sauce, sugar and hot sauce. Add the frankfurters and simmer for 10 minutes, stirring occasionally. Cook the noodles according to package directions and drain. Place the frankfurters in center of a heated platter and surround with the noodles. 6 servings.

Mrs. Bernice J. Bennett, Kosciusko, Mississippi

Liver Loaf with Bacon (below)

LIVER LOAF WITH BACON
Easily prepared; allow 1 hour for cooking

1/2 c. bread crumbs	1 tbsp. lemon juice
1 c. milk	1 tsp. salt
1 1/2 lb. liver	Dash of white pepper
3/4 lb. ground pork	Dash of paprika
1 egg	1/2 lb. sliced bacon
2 tbsp. dried onion	Tomato Sauce
2 tbsp. tomato soup	

Place the bread crumbs in a small bowl and add the milk. Grind the liver in a food chopper, then mix with the ground pork, egg, onion, tomato soup, lemon juice and seasonings. Add the moistened bread crumbs and mix well. Shape into a loaf and place the bacon slices around the loaf. Place in an oiled loaf pan. Bake at 350 degrees for 1 hour. Turn out the hot loaf on a serving platter and garnish with slices of pepper and tomatoes. Serve with Tomato Sauce.

Tomato Sauce

1 can tomatoes	1/4 tsp. white pepper
1/2 tsp. garlic salt	

Press the tomatoes through a sieve into a saucepan and add the seasonings. Simmer for 5 minutes. Serve hot with the liver loaf.

SPANISH SWEETBREADS
Preparation and cooking time less than 1 hour

2 c. sliced sweetbreads
Salt and pepper to taste
Flour
1 sm. can tomatoes

1/2 med. onion, chopped
1 jalapeno pepper, chopped
1/2 c. water

Season the sweetbreads with salt and pepper and dredge with flour. Brown in a skillet in small amount of fat. Combine the tomatoes, onion, pepper and water in a saucepan and bring to a boil. Pour over the sweetbreads and simmer for 20 minutes. 6 servings.

Mrs. Ruth Klose, Haskell, Texas

GRILLED FRANKFURTERS WITH SAUERKRAUT
Preparation and cooking time less than 1 hour

1 can sauerkraut
1/2 c. bouillon

1 tbsp. margarine
1 pkg. frankfurters

Rinse the sauerkraut and drain. Boil the sauerkraut and bouillon, covered, over low heat for about 40 minutes. Melt the margarine in a frypan. Cut small crosses in the frankfurters and fry in the melted margarine over low heat until slightly browned. Bend the frankfurters in horseshoe shapes and arrange over the hot sauerkraut in a serving bowl. Serve with mustard and brown bread.

Grilled Frankfurters with Sauerkraut (above)

MUSHROOMS WITH LAMB
Elegant but quickly prepared; 30 minutes for cooking

8 thin slices lamb	6 tbsp. butter
8 oz. canned mushrooms	2 tbsp. flour
1 tsp. chopped parsley	1 tbsp. lemon juice

Place the lamb in a saucepan. Add enough hot water to cover the lamb and let soak for 10 minutes. Saute the mushrooms and parsley in the butter in a skillet until mushrooms are tender, then remove from skillet and set aside. Drain the lamb and dredge with the flour. Fry in butter remaining in the skillet until browned. Add the mushroom mixture and lemon juice and heat through. 3 servings.

Mrs. John Beaulieu, Orlando, Florida

GROUND LAMB CURRY
Partially prepared ahead; allow 1 hour for baking

2 lb. ground lamb	1 tsp. basil
1/2 c. chopped onion	1/2 c. chopped celery
1 c. chopped tomatoes	1/2 lb. sliced mushrooms
1 tsp. oregano	1 recipe pie pastry

Place the ground lamb and onion in a skillet and cook until browned, stirring frequently. Add the tomatoes and herbs and heat thoroughly. Place in a large baking dish and add the celery and mushrooms. Cover with pie crust. Bake at 350 degrees for 1 hour.

Mrs. Annie Lee A. Glover, Lynchburg, South Carolina

LAMB PATTIES WITH CURRANT-ORANGE SAUCE
20 minutes to prepare; 20 minutes to cook

1 1/2 lb. ground lamb	1/4 tsp. marjoram
1 c. soft bread crumbs	1 egg, well beaten
1/4 c. milk	1/2 c. red currant jelly
1 tsp. salt	1/2 tsp. grated orange rind

Combine the lamb, bread crumbs, milk, salt, marjoram and egg in a mixing bowl and mix well. Shape in 3/4-inch thick patties and place in a shallow baking pan. Broil for 8 to 10 minutes. Turn patties and broil until brown. Heat the jelly in a small saucepan until melted and add orange rind. Serve over patties.

Myrtle M. Stafford, West Liberty, Kentucky

PENNSYLVANIA DUTCH BURGERS
Preparation and cooking time less than 30 minutes

1/2 lb. ground ham	1/4 c. fine dry bread crumbs
1/2 lb. ground pork	1 egg, slightly beaten

1/4 tsp. dry mustard | 1 can brown gravy with onions
Dash of ground cloves | 4 apple rings, 1/2 inch thick

Combine the ham, pork, bread crumbs, egg, mustard and cloves and mix well. Shape into 4 patties. Brown the patties in a skillet, then pour off the fat and add the gravy. Cover and cook over low heat for 30 minutes. Top the patties with the apple rings. Cover and cook for 15 minutes longer, stirring occasionally. 4 servings.

Photograph for this recipe on page 42.

GLAZED HAM
Fancy yet easy to prepare; allow about 1 hour and 30 minutes to bake

1   9-lb. (about) canned ham | 1 tbsp. angostura aromatic
1   11-oz. can mandarin oranges | bitters
1 tbsp. cornstarch | 1 tbsp. cider vinegar
1/2 c. orange marmalade | 1/2 tsp. ground cloves
1 tsp. dry mustard | Whole cloves

Remove the ham from the can and place on a rack in a shallow roasting pan. Drain the oranges and mix the juice slowly into the cornstarch in a saucepan. Add the orange marmalade, mustard, angostura bitters, vinegar and ground cloves. Cook over low heat, stirring constantly, until thickened. Score the top of the ham in a diamond pattern with a sharp knife. Bake at 350 degrees for 1 hour. Brush the ham top and sides with the angostura bitters glaze. Bake for 30 minutes longer brushing glaze over the ham several times. Remove from oven and decorate the top with the orange sections and whole cloves. Spoon remaining glaze lightly over the sections. Bake for 5 minutes longer. 12-15 servings.

Glazed Ham (above)

FRIED HAM SLICES
Allow 30 minutes for marinating; prepared and cooked in 30 minutes

3 slices country ham, cut into halves	1/2 c. flour
1 c. milk	1 tbsp. fat

Place the ham in a shallow dish and cover with the milk. Let stand for 30 minutes. Remove from milk and roll in the flour. Melt the fat in a heavy skillet and cook ham over low heat until tender and browned on both sides. 6 servings.

Mrs. Bess Snyder Mohl, Petersburg, West Virginia

PORK CHOP DISH
20 minutes to prepare; 20 minutes to bake

2 tbsp. fat	1 lge. white onion
8 pork chops	2 fresh green sweet peppers
Salt and pepper to taste	2 lge. fresh tomatoes, sliced

Place the fat in a large skillet. Add the pork chops and brown on both sides. Season with salt and pepper. Cut the onion in thin slices and slice the peppers into rings. Place an onion slice, a pepper ring and tomato slice on each chop. Salt again lightly. Cover skillet tightly and cook at 275 degrees for 20 minutes. Add water if chops become too dry. 8 servings.

Mrs. J. J. Durham, Hereford, Texas

PORK CHOPS IN RICE
Prepared and cooked in about 1 hour

4 pork chops	3/4 soup can water
Salt and pepper to taste	1 box long grain and wild rice
1 can golden mushroom soup	

Brown the pork chops in a small amount of fat and season with salt and pepper. Combine the mushroom soup, water, rice mix and seasonings included in mix and heat. Pour over the pork chops and simmer for about 1 hour or until tender. 4 servings.

Mrs. Rhonda Mills, Goldsboro, North Carolina

BREADED PORK CHOPS WITH APPLE RINGS
Preparation and cooking time less than 1 hour

1 egg	1 c. cracker crumbs
1 tsp. salt	1/4 c. shortening
1/4 tsp. pepper	3 to 4 unpeeled apples
4 pork chops, 1/2 in. thick	

Mix the egg, 2 tablespoons water and seasonings and dip the pork chops into egg mixture. Roll in the crumbs and let stand for several minutes. Brown chops on both sides in hot shortening. Cover and cook over low heat for 30 minutes. Remove from pan and keep warm. Core the apples and cut into 1/2-inch slices. Fry the apple slices in the same pan until tender and lightly browned. 4 servings.

Mrs. Mary Ruth Wilson, Knoxville, Tennessee

Baked Sausage with Creamed Mushrooms (below)

BAKED SAUSAGE WITH CREAMED MUSHROOMS
Preparation and cooking time about 30 minutes

1 1-lb. sausage roll	1 c. milk
1 pkg. frozen broccoli, thawed	1 can sliced mushrooms
2 tbsp. margarine	1/4 c. chili sauce
3 tbsp. flour	

Cut the sausage in thin slices and arrange, overlapping in 3 rows in a greased baking dish. Place the broccoli between the sausage rows. Melt the margarine in a saucepan, then stir in the flour. Add the milk gradually, stirring constantly. Add the the mushrooms and boil for 5 minutes, stirring until sauce is smooth. Distribute the creamed mushrooms over sausage and broccoli. Spoon the chili sauce in stripes across the sausage. Bake at 350 degrees for 15 minutes.

VEAL FRICASSEE
Prepared and cooked in about 1 hour

2 lb. veal steak, 1/2 in. thick	1 tsp. paprika
Salt and pepper to taste	1 c. sour cream
Flour	1/2 c. meat stock or water

Cut the veal steak into serving pieces and season with salt and pepper. Dredge with flour and brown in a small amount of hot fat in a skillet. Combine 1 tablespoon flour, paprika, sour cream and stock and mix well. Pour over veal and cover. Cook over low heat for 1 hour. 6 servings.

Mrs. T. J. Clanton, Jr., Buckatunna, Mississippi

VEAL PARMESAN
Prepared and cooked in 1 hour

2 tsp. margarine or oil	1/2 tsp. salt
4 veal steaks, 1/2 in. thick	Dash of pepper
5/8 c. grated Parmesan cheese	2/3 c. evaporated milk
1/4 c. flour	1 8-oz. can tomato sauce

Preheat oven to 350 degrees. Melt the margarine in a 12 x 8-inch pan in oven. Mix 2 tablespoons Parmesan cheese, flour, salt and pepper. Dip the veal in 1/3 cup evaporated milk, then roll in cheese mixture. Place in prepared pan. Bake for 30 minutes. Mix remaining milk and Parmesan cheese. Remove veal from oven and pour tomato sauce around veal. Spoon cheese mixture on veal and bake 20 to 25 minutes longer or until veal is tender. 4 servings.

Mrs. Hilda Coufal, Hungerford, Texas

EASY EXECUTIVE'S DINNER

Veal Parmesan *page 60*
Marinated Green Bean Salad *page 35*
Parslied Potatoes *page 107*
Parker House Rolls *page 182*
Cold Lemon Souffle *page 156*

BRAISED VEAL STEAK WITH MUSHROOMS
Preparation and cooking time about 1 hour

1 egg, slightly beaten	2 c. crushed cereal flakes
2 tbsp. milk	4 tbsp. fat
2 lb. veal steak, 1 in. thick	1 sm. can mushrooms

Combine the egg and milk and mix well. Cut the steak into serving pieces, dip into the egg mixture and roll in cereal flakes. Brown in hot fat in a skillet, then cover with the mushrooms and liquid. Cover tightly. Cook over low heat for about 45 minutes or until tender. Thicken liquid for gravy, if desired, and serve with veal steaks. 6 servings.

Martha Coats, Bivins, Texas

VEAL PAPRIKA
Allow 1 hour for marinating; prepared and cooked in 30 minutes

1 lb. thinly sliced veal	Flour
3 tbsp. lemon juice	1/2 pt. sour cream
5 onions, sliced	1 c. beef stock
Butter	Salt and pepper to taste
1 tbsp. paprika	

Marinate the veal slices in lemon juice for 1 hour. Saute the onions in a skillet in small amount of butter until light brown and sprinkle with paprika. Dredge the veal with flour and brown in a small amount of butter in a separate skillet. Place on the onions and cover the skillet. Cook over low heat for 5 to 6 minutes. Mix 1 tablespoon flour with the sour cream, then stir in the stock, salt and pepper. Pour over the veal and cook for 5 minutes longer.

Mrs. Remmington McConnell, Atlanta, Georgia

CHEESE-BAKED VEAL FARCE
Easily prepared; allow about 1 hour and 15 minutes for baking

1 lb. ground veal	1/3 c. cream
1/4 lb. ground pork	1 potato, boiled and mashed
1 egg yolk	1/2 pkg. sliced bacon
Salt and pepper to taste	3 slices Cheddar cheese
2/3 c. water	

Combine the veal, pork, egg yolk, seasonings, water, cream and the mashed potato and blend well. Shape into a roll and place in a greased baking pan. Cover the roll with bacon slices. Bake at 350 degrees for about 1 hour. Cut the roll in even slices. Cut each cheese slice in 4 triangles and insert a cheese slice between each meat roll slice. Bake at 450 degrees until cheese melts. Serve with tomatoes, broccoli, boiled potatoes, gravy sauce and a green salad.

Cheese-Baked Veal Farce (above)

poultry

Versatile poultry — southern homemakers appreciate the way its mild taste and smooth texture mix and match with the entire delightful spectrum of food flavors. They also know that poultry — especially that all-time southern favorite, chicken — can often be prepared quickly and easily.

The section that follows features favorite, home-tested poultry recipes from kitchens throughout the Southland, chosen especially for their ease of preparation. Some are traditional fare you'll depend on for tasty, hearty family meals — recipes like Lazy Barbecue . . . Chicken Paprika . . . Chicken with Noodles . . . or Turkey with Orange Rice. Others are gourmet poultry dishes you'll proudly serve on any special occasion. Imagine, for example, offering your family and guests elegant — but oh-so-easy — Chicken a la King. Or cook Italian style and feature Chicken Tetrazzini as your center of attraction.

These recipes — like all of the others in this section — have had the work pared out of them. But the flavor excitement stays! These are much-praised, delicious dishes which reflect the fine art of cooking at its best — and most efficient. They all look and taste as if they were the products of hours in the kitchen . . . and only you know better. Explore this section now, and begin bringing the benefits of quick and easy poultry to your dining table!

Stuffed Broiler (below)

STUFFED BROILER
Preparation and cooking time about 1 hour and 30 minutes

1 2 to 3-lb. broiler	1 med. yellow onion
Salt	Margarine
Freshly ground pepper	1/2 tsp. curry
2 or 3 tart apples	

Rinse and wipe the broiler dry, then season inside with salt and pepper. Pare and core the apples and cut in large cubes. Coarsely chop the onion, then saute the apples and onion in a small amount of margarine until golden, but not brown. Spoon the apples and onion into the broiler cavity. Fasten the neck skin to the body with a skewer and tie the legs together with string. Place on a rack in a roasting pan and rub with several pats of margarine. Bake at 350 degrees for about 1 hour. Melt 2 tablespoons margarine in a saucepan and add the curry, 1/2 teaspoon salt and a dash of pepper. Brush the broiler with the curry butter. Bake for 15 minutes longer, or until golden brown, brushing frequently. Remove the broiler to a serving platter and add water or chicken stock to the pan. Cook and stir over low heat until the pan drippings are blended with the liquid, then strain. Carve the broiler and serve with the filling, gravy and curried rice.

GRILLED CHICKEN WITH SPICED SAUCE
Preparation and cooking time about 1 hour

1 broiler chicken	1 tbsp. soy sauce
Salt and pepper to taste	Juice of 1/2 lemon
2 tbsp. butter	

Rub the chicken with salt and pepper, then place on a rack in a broiler pan. Broil about 5 inches from source of heat until chicken is tender. Melt the butter in a saucepan, then add the soy sauce and lemon juice and bring to a boil. Add about 1/2 cup water and bring to a boil again. Cut the broiler in serving pieces and arrange on a platter. Garnish with green pepper rings, if desired. Serve the sauce over the chicken or in a sauceboat.

Photograph for this recipe on page 62.

BRANDIED CHICKEN BREASTS
Elegant but quickly prepared; 45 minutes for cooking

6 chicken breasts	1/4 c. brandy
2 tbsp. butter	1/2 tsp. salt
2 cans cream of mushroom soup	1/4 tsp. pepper
1 can mushrooms	Dash of hot sauce
1 bay leaf	1/4 tsp. cayenne pepper

Saute the chicken in the butter in a skillet until lightly browned. Add the mushroom soup, mushrooms, bay leaf, brandy, salt, pepper, hot sauce and cayenne and cover. Cook over low heat until tender. Remove and discard the bay leaf. Serve over rice or mashed potatoes, if desired. 6 servings.

Mrs. Paul E. Johnson, Oklahoma City, Oklahoma

CHICKEN A LA KING
Quick leftovers dividend; 30 minutes cooking time

1/4 c. chopped onion	1 1/3 c. cooked cubed chicken
2 tbsp. chopped green pepper	2 tbsp. diced pimento
2 tbsp. margarine	Dash of pepper
1 can cream of mushroom soup	4 frozen waffles, toasted
1/3 c. milk	

Cook the onion and green pepper in the margarine until tender. Blend in the soup and milk, then add the chicken, pimento and pepper. Heat over low heat, stirring frequently. Serve over toasted waffles. 4 servings.

Mrs. Linda Green, Greenwood, Mississippi

QUICK CHICKEN LUNCHEON MENU

Chicken a la King *page 65*
Cheese Broccoli *page 102*
Tomato Salad *page 36*

CHICKEN AND MACARONI
Emergency shelf ingredients; mix and bake for 1 hour

1 can cream of chicken soup	
Milk	1 12-oz. can chicken, diced
1 1/2 c. cooked elbow macaroni	1 c. sliced canned mushrooms
2 c. grated Cheddar cheese	1/4 c. diced pimento

Combine the soup and enough milk to measure 2 cups. Mix all the ingredients together and pour into a buttered 2-quart baking dish. Bake at 350 degrees for 1 hour. 6-8 servings.

Mrs. M. H. Mohr, Gretna, Louisiana

CHICKEN HUNTINGTON
Partially prepared ahead; allow 30 minutes for cooking

1 5-lb. chicken	2 sm. cans pimentos
1 c. macaroni	1 can English peas
4 tbsp. flour	1 can mushrooms
1 c. cubed cheese	Salt and pepper

Cook the chicken in boiling water until tender. Drain and reserve 2 cups broth. Bone the chicken and cut in small pieces. Cook the macaroni according to package directions and drain. Place the flour in a saucepan and add reserved broth slowly. Cook, stirring, until thickened. Add the chicken, macaroni, cheese, pimentos, peas, mushrooms, salt and pepper and mix. Place in a greased baking dish. Bake at 350 degrees for about 30 minutes.

Mrs. W. W. Briant, Shallowater, Texas

CHARLIE'S DO-IT-YOURSELF DINNER
Emergency shelf ingredients; mix and cook for 40 minutes

1 can boned chicken	1/8 tsp. marjoram
2 cans cream of celery soup	1 pkg. lasagna noodles, cooked
1 can shrimp soup	1/2 c. (or more) Parmesan
1 green pepper, diced	cheese
1 can peas, drained	1/4 lb. butter
1 c. sour cream	1/2 c. milk
Salt and pepper to taste	1/2 c. bread crumbs

Mix chicken, soups, green pepper, peas, sour cream, salt, pepper and marjoram together. Place a layer of noodles in a buttered baking dish. Sprinkle with a portion of the cheese and dot with butter. Cover with a layer of soup mixture. Add cheese and butter. Repeat until layer ingredients are used, ending with noodle layer topped with cheese. Pour the milk over the top and sprinkle with crumbs and cheese. Bake at 350 degrees for 40 minutes. 8 servings.

Mrs. Emmet Rice, Georgetown, Delaware

CHICKEN AND NOODLES
Preparation and cooking time less than 1 hour

1 pkg. broad noodles	1 sm. can pimento
1 c. chicken broth	1 can mushrooms
3/4 c. flour	1 No. 303 can English peas
1 1/2 pt. thick cream	Bread crumbs
1 5-lb. cooked hen	

Cook the noodles in boiling, salted water for 5 minutes and drain. Add the broth to flour in a saucepan slowly, stirring constantly. Stir in the cream and cook until thick, stirring constantly. Remove from heat and stir in the noodles. Remove chicken from bones and dice. Stir into noodle mixture. Mix in remaining ingredients except bread crumbs and place in a greased baking dish. Cover with bread crumbs. Bake at 350 degrees for 30 minutes. 12 servings.

Mrs. Mildred Tate, Henderson, Kentucky

CHICKEN SUPREME
Prepared and cooked in 1 hour

2 c. noodles	1/2 tsp. sage
1 c. diced chicken	1 tsp. salt
1/2 c. sour cream	1/2 tsp. pepper
1 can cream of chicken soup	

Cook the noodles according to package directions until almost done and tender. Combine all the ingredients in a baking dish. Bake for 30 to 40 minutes at 350 degrees. Serve hot. 6 servings.

Mrs. Rochelle Newcomb, Enid, Oklahoma

CHICKEN PAPRIKASH
Partially prepared ahead; allow 1 hour for cooking

1/4 c. butter	1/4 tsp. pepper
1 3 1/2-lb. frying chicken, cut-up	1 13 3/4-oz. can chicken broth
1/2 c. chopped onion	2 c. sour cream
1/4 c. flour	1 tbsp. Worcestershire sauce
2 tbsp. paprika	1 8-oz. package medium noodles, cooked and drained
2 tsp. salt	

Melt the butter in a large frypan. Saute the chicken pieces until lightly browned, then remove from the pan and add the onion to the pan drippings. Blend in the flour, paprika, salt and pepper. Add the chicken broth and cook, stirring constantly, until thick and smooth. Stir in the sour cream and Worcestershire sauce. Mix 1/2 of the sauce with the noodles and pour into a shallow 3-quart casserole. Arrange the chicken pieces on the noodles. Spoon remaining sauce over the chicken pieces. Bake at 325 degrees for about 1 hour or until chicken is tender and noodles are hot. 6 servings.

Chicken Paprikash (above)

BAKED CHICKEN AND RICE
Quick leftovers dividend; 30 minutes cooking time

2 c. cooked rice	1 c. clear broth
2 c. diced chicken	Salt and pepper to taste

Combine rice, chicken, broth and seasonings and place in an 8-inch baking dish. Bake at 350 degrees until brown. 4 servings.

Mrs. Lillian C. Lanham, Binger, Oklahoma

CHICKEN AND RICE
20 minutes to prepare; 20 minutes to bake

1 c. chopped celery	3 hard-cooked eggs, chopped
1 can cream of chicken soup	1 c. cooked rice
1/2 c. chopped almonds	1 can boned chicken
2 tbsp. chopped onion	2 c. crushed potato chips
3/4 c. mayonnaise	

Cook the celery in a small amount of water until tender, then combine with the soup, almonds, onion, mayonnaise and eggs. Alternate layers of rice, chicken and soup mixture in a buttered casserole and top with potato chips. Bake at 400 degrees for 20 minutes. 6-8 servings.

Mrs. Barbara Rogers, Meridian, Mississippi

CHICKEN HAVALANTA
Elegant but quickly prepared; 30 minutes for cooking

Butter	1 pkg. yellow rice
4 green onions, chopped	1 tsp. salt
1 3-lb. chicken, cut up	2 bananas

Melt 1/2 stick butter in a skillet and add the onions. Place the chicken in the butter mixture and brown lightly. Add the rice and cook until slightly brown. Cover the chicken and rice with water and add the salt. Bring to a boil, then cover and reduce heat. Cook for about 25 minutes. Slice the bananas and brown in about 4 tablespoons butter. Spoon the chicken and rice on a platter and garnish with the banana slices.

Lila Stanley Benton, Atlanta, Georgia

CHICKEN HAWAIIAN
Elegant but quickly prepared; 30 minutes for cooking

1 13-oz. can pineapple tidbits	2 cans cream of chicken soup
1 lge. green pepper, cut	2 c. cubed cooked chicken
2 cloves of garlic, minced	2 tbsp. soy sauce
2 tbsp. salad oil	3 c. cooked rice
	1/4 c. toasted slivered almonds

Drain the pineapple, reserving juice. Cook the green pepper and garlic in the oil in a saucepan until tender. Blend in the soup and 1/2 cup pineapple juice. Add the chicken, pineapple and soy sauce. Heat and stir. Serve over rice and top with almonds. 6 servings.

Lillian Dunn, Lufkin, Texas

CHICKEN STUFFING BAKE
Elegant but easily prepared; 45 minutes for cooking

1   8-oz. package seasoned
stuffing mix
2 1/2 lb. frying chicken pieces
1 env. seasoned coating mix
for chicken

1   16-oz. can peeled whole
apricots, drained
1/3 c. flaked coconut
Onion Sauce

Prepare the stuffing mix according to package directions and spoon into bottom of a large shallow casserole. Coat the chicken with the seasoned coating mix according to package directions. Arrange chicken in a single layer over the dressing. Bake at 400 degrees for 20 minutes, then remove from oven. Arrange the apricots around sides of the casserole, then sprinkle with coconut. Bake for 20 to 25 minutes longer or until the chicken is tender. Serve with Onion Sauce. 6 servings.

Onion Sauce

1 1/2 c. sliced onions
1/4 c. butter
1 c. chicken broth
3/4 tsp. salt

2 tbsp. all-purpose flour
1 tsp. paprika
1/2 c. sour cream
1/4 c. milk

Saute the onions in the butter until tender, but not browned. Add the chicken broth and salt and simmer for about 30 minutes. Blend the flour with the paprika and sour cream and stir into the onion mixture. Add the milk and stir over low heat until heated thoroughly. Do not boil.

Chicken Stuffing Bake (above)

CHICKEN AND SHRIMP
Emergency shelf ingredients; mix and bake for 1 hour

1 can boned chicken	1 c. diced Velveeta cheese
1 can cream of shrimp soup	Seasoned bread crumbs
1 soup can milk	

Mix the chicken, soup, milk and cheese and pour into a baking dish. Top with bread crumbs. Bake at 350 degrees for 1 hour.

Mrs. Hilda Keever, Baltimore, Maryland

CHICKEN BREAST GOURMET
Elegant but quickly prepared; 30 minutes for cooking

4 chicken breasts	1 c. white cooking wine
1/4 c. butter	1 c. sour cream
1/2 white onion, chopped	

Brown the chicken breasts in butter in a skillet, then add the onion and wine. Cook over low heat for 15 minutes and remove breasts. Pour the sour cream into the pan and stir till blended. Pour sour cream mixture over the chicken and serve. 4 servings.

Mrs. M. L. Ancelman, Covington, Kentucky

CHICKEN CRUNCH
Quick leftovers dividend; 30 minutes cooking time

1 3 1/2-oz. can French-fried onions	2 cans cream of mushroom soup
2 c. cooked diced chicken	1 5-oz. can chow mein noodles
1 c. finely cut celery	1 5-oz. can water chestnuts, sliced

Reserve a few onions for the topping. Mix remaining onions, chicken, celery, soup, noodles and chestnuts and place in a baking dish. Top with reserved onions. Bake at 350 degrees for 30 minutes. 6 servings.

Mrs. Pierre N. Canese, Southport, North Carolina

CHICKEN MARENGO
Prepared and cooked in 1 hour

3 lb. chicken parts	1 can tomato soup
3 tbsp. shortening	1 clove of garlic, minced
1 can golden mushroom soup	1 lb. small white onions

Brown the chicken in shortening in a large skillet and pour off shortening. Add remaining ingredients and cover. Simmer for 45 minutes or until the chicken is tender, stirring occasionally. Add water, if necessary. Uncover and cook to desired consistency. 6 servings.

Mrs. Marybeth Windsor, Madisonville, Tennessee

CHICKEN PAPRIKA
Fancy, yet easy to prepare; allow 1 hour for cooking

4 lb. chicken parts	1/2 c. chopped onion
1/2 c. seasoned flour	2 4-oz. cans sliced mushrooms
1/3 c. shortening	1 tbsp. paprika
2 cans tomato soup	1 lge. bay leaf
1/2 c. water	1 c. sour cream

Coat the chicken with seasoned flour and brown in the shortening in a large skillet. Pour off fat and stir in remaining ingredients except sour cream. Cover. Simmer for 45 minutes or until tender, stirring occasionally. Remove bay leaf and stir in the sour cream. Heat through. Serve with noodles. 8-10 servings.

Mrs. Paulette Meeks, Broken Bow, Oklahoma

CHICKEN DIVAN PARISIAN
Preparation and cooking time less than 1 hour

1 can cream of celery soup	1 tsp. Worcestershire sauce
1/4 c. milk	2 pkg. frozen broccoli
1/4 tsp. nutmeg	2 c. sliced cooked chicken
1 c. heavy cream	1 c. grated Parmesan cheese
1/2 c. mayonnaise	

Mix the soup, milk and nutmeg in a saucepan and heat through. Combine the cream, mayonnaise and Worcestershire sauce and stir in the soup mixture. Cook the broccoli according to package directions and place in a shallow casserole in a single layer. Spoon half the soup mixture over broccoli. Cover with chicken slices and add remaining soup mixture. Sprinkle with cheese. Bake at 350 degrees for 20 minutes or until bubbly. 6-8 servings.

Mrs. W. Murray Smith, Clay, West Virginia

POPOVER PIE
Partially prepared ahead; allow 15 minutes for baking

1 3-lb. cooked chicken	2 tbsp. baking powder
3 tbsp. melted butter	1 egg, beaten
2 3/8 c. flour	1 c. coffee cream
3 c. warm broth	2 tsp. butter
1 tsp. salt	

Remove chicken from bones and cut in large pieces. Place in a deep baking pan. Combine the melted butter and 3/8 cup flour in a saucepan. Add the broth gradually and cook, stirring constantly, until thick. Pour over chicken. Combine remaining flour, salt and baking powder in a bowl. Mix the egg and cream and stir into flour mixture. Drop by spoonfuls over chicken mixture and dot with butter. Bake in 350-degree oven for 15 minutes or until crust is brown.

Mrs. Clara Smith, New Orleans, Louisiana

Sesame-Fried Chicken (below)

SESAME-FRIED CHICKEN
Easily prepared; allow 45 minutes for cooking

1 3-lb. broiler-fryer chicken, cut up	1 tbsp. seasoned salt
1 env. instant mashed potato granules	2 eggs
	1 c. sesame seed

Place the chicken on a rack in a large saucepan and pour over 1 cup water. Bring to a boil, then cover tightly and steam for 20 to 25 minutes. Shake the steamed chicken in a paper bag containing instant potato granules and seasoned salt. Beat the eggs and 2 tablespoons water together. Dip the chicken in the egg mixture, then roll in the sesame seed. Shake again in the potato mixture and allow to stand for about 10 minutes to let coating set. Fry in deep 365-degree shortening for about 3 to 5 minutes or until brown and crisp. Drain on paper towels before serving. 4 servings.

CHICKEN SUB GUM
Emergency shelf ingredients; mix and cook for 20 minutes

2 c. cooked diced chicken	2 c. diced celery
2 tbsp. chopped onion	1 can cream of chicken soup
1 can mushrooms	1 can bean sprouts

Blend all the ingredients in a saucepan and cook until heated through. Serve hot over Chinese noodles or rice. One cup chicken broth may be substituted for the soup. 4-5 servings.

Mrs. Dawson Richey, New Castle, Delaware

CHICKEN SPAGHETTI
Quick leftovers dividend; 20 minutes cooking time

2 c. chopped cooked chicken	2 whole cloves
2 c. consomme or broth	3 tbsp. mushrooms
1/2 c. tomato soup	3/4 tsp. salt
3/4 clove of garlic, chopped	3/4 c. broken spaghetti
3 tbsp. chopped onion	

Combine the chicken, consomme, soup, garlic, onion and cloves in a saucepan. Add the mushrooms and cook over moderate heat for 10 minutes. Season with salt. Add the spaghetti and boil for 10 minutes or until tender. Serve hot. 6 servings.

Mary Jo Baty, Shelbyville, Texas

CHICKEN TETRAZZINI
Partially prepared ahead; allow 20 minutes for baking

2 5-lb. cooked hens	6 tbsp. margarine
1/2 tsp. salt	9 tbsp. flour
1 lge. can mushroom soup	3 c. chicken stock
1 c. grapes	1 c. cream
1 sm. jar pimento strips	1 c. grated cheese
1/2 c. blanched almonds	1 can Chinese noodles

Remove chicken from bones and cut in large pieces. Add the salt, soup, grapes, pimento and almonds. Melt the margarine in a saucepan. Add flour and stir until blended. Add stock slowly and bring to a boil, stirring constantly. Cook for 2 minutes and remove from heat. Stir in cream and mix with the chicken mixture. Place in a greased baking dish and cover with cheese. Bake at 400 degrees until lightly browned and serve over noodles.

Mrs. J. P. La Groon, McCormick, South Carolina

CHICKEN WITH ARTICHOKES
Partially prepared ahead; allow 30 minutes for baking

1 tbsp. (heaping) butter	1/4 tsp. ground mace
1 cut-up fried chicken	1/2 c. dry sherry
1 jar artichoke hearts	2/3 c. light cream
1 can cream of chicken soup	1 can mushrooms
1 tsp. poultry seasoning	

Place the butter in a roasting pan and arrange fried chicken over it. Arrange the artichoke hearts over chicken. Mix remaining ingredients, then pour over top and cover. Bake for 30 minutes in a 350-degree oven. Garnish with parsley, if desired. 4 servings.

Mrs. Willis D. Holland, Edgewood, Maryland

CHICKEN WITH CHEESE AND SHERRY SAUCE
Prepared and cooked in 1 hour

Boned chicken breasts	Melted margarine
Salt and pepper to taste	Grated sharp Cheddar cheese
Oregano to taste	1/2 c. sherry

Season the chicken with salt, pepper and oregano. Dip in the margarine and arrange the chicken in layer in a shallow baking dish. Bake for 45 minutes in 350-degree oven. Chicken should be golden brown. Remove from oven. Sprinkle with grated cheese. Pour sherry over the cheese and return to oven. Bake for 15 minutes longer.

Mrs. Reuben Preston, Williamsburg, Kentucky

EASY PERFECTION LUNCHEON

Chicken with Cheese and Sherry Sauce *page 74*
Mixed Vegetable Salad *page 35*
Mystery Muffins *page 181*
Coffee Mallo *page 156*

ORANGE MARMALADE-CURRY CHICKEN
Elegant but quickly prepared, 45 minutes for cooking

4 chicken breasts, thighs or drumsticks	1/2 c. orange marmalade
Flour	1/2 c. warm water
Butter	1/2 tsp. (or more) curry powder
	Salt and pepper to taste

Roll the chicken pieces in flour and brown in a small amount of butter in a frying pan. Mix marmalade, water, curry powder and seasonings and baste the chicken pieces, then pour the remaining marmalade mixture into the frying pan and cover. Cook for 30 minutes or until chicken is tender. Remove cover and cook for 5 minutes longer. 4 servings.

Mrs. Ronald A. Stephens, Waco, Texas

ITALIAN CHICKEN
Preparation and cooking time about 1 hour

1/2 c. salad oil	1 pkg. spaghetti sauce mix
1 2 to 3-lb. fryer, cut up	1 1/2 c. sauterne
1 tsp. seasoned salt	1 8-oz. can tomato sauce
1 tsp. monosodium glutamate	3 tbsp. instant minced onions
1 tsp. pepper	1 4-oz. can sliced mushrooms

Heat the oil in a skillet to 400 degrees. Sprinkle the chicken with seasoned salt, monosodium glutamate and pepper and brown in the hot oil. Add remaining ingredients and stir. Cover and simmer for 45 minutes or until chicken is tender. 6 servings.

Mrs. O. C. Newhall, Hagerstown, Maryland

COMPANY CHICKEN BREASTS
Elegant but quickly prepared; 1 hour and 30 minutes for cooking

8 chicken breasts	2 cans cream of mushroom soup
Salt and pepper to taste	2 c. cream
Paprika to taste	

Season the chicken with salt, pepper and paprika and place in single layer in a greased shallow baking pan. Mix the mushroom soup and cream in a bowl and spoon over the chicken. Bake at 350 degrees for about 1 hour and 30 minutes. 6 servings.

Mrs. Willie D. Morrison, Cave City, Kentucky

LAZY BARBECUE
Preparation and cooking time less than 1 hour

1 6 1/2-oz. bottle cola beverage	Garlic salt to taste
1 c. catsup	1 med. chicken, disjointed
1 tbsp. Worcestershire sauce	

Place all the ingredients in a large skillet and cover. Simmer for 45 minutes to 1 hour or until the chicken is tender. Serve with rice. 6 servings.

Mrs. R. C. Cadden, Jr., Aberdeen, Mississippi

QUICK CREAMED CHICKEN
Quick leftovers dividend; 20 minutes cooking time

1 can cream of mushroom soup	1 pimento, diced
1/4 c. milk	1/4 c. chopped celery
2 c. diced cooked chicken	

Combine the soup and milk in a saucepan and heat, stirring constantly. Add the chicken, pimento and celery and cook for several minutes to blend flavors. Serve on toast or on split corn bread squares. 4-6 servings.

Mrs. H. O. Newton, Quincy, Florida

CHICKEN TIMBALES
Preparation and cooking time about 1 hour

2 c. diced cooked chicken	1 14-oz. can mushrooms, drained
3/4 tsp. salt	1 1/2 c. milk
1/4 tsp. pepper	3/4 c. chopped celery
1 tbsp. Worcestershire sauce	1 c. oats
2 eggs, beaten	

Combine all ingredients and place in greased custard cups. Bake at 350 degrees for about 50 minutes. Serve with mushroom sauce, if desired. 6 servings.

Mrs. Annie Ruth Smith, McColl, South Carolina

QUICK OVEN CHICKEN
Preparation and cooking time less than 1 hour

1 c. bread crumbs	1/8 tsp. pepper
1/4 c. grated Parmesan cheese	1/2 c. butter
2 tbsp. minced parsley	1 clove of garlic, crushed
1 tsp. salt	2 1/2 lb. chicken pieces
1/4 tsp. thyme	

Combine the bread crumbs, cheese, parsley, salt, thyme and pepper. Melt the butter in a frypan and stir in the garlic. Dip the chicken in the butter mixture and coat with the crumb mixture. Place in a foil-lined baking pan. Bake at 400 degrees for 45 minutes or until the chicken is tender. Do not turn chicken. 4-6 servings.

Mrs. Goz Segars, Jr., Hartsville, South Carolina

SUCCULENT CHICKEN STEW WITH CHIVE DUMPLINGS
20 minutes to prepare; 20 minutes to cook

2 cans chicken stew	3/4 c. milk
2 c. packaged biscuit mix	3 tbsp. frozen chives

Heat the stew to boiling point in electric skillet. Mix the biscuit mix, milk and chives with a fork. Drop by spoonfuls onto boiling stew. Cook, uncovered, on low heat for 10 minutes, then cover and cook for 10 minutes longer. 5-6 servings.

Mrs. Dorothy M. Duncan, Dalton, Georgia

SEVEN-MINUTE CHICKEN DISH
Quick leftovers dividend; 7 minutes cooking time

1 can cream of mushroom soup	1 1/2 c. diced chicken
1 can cream of celery soup	1 1/3 c. packaged precooked rice
1 soup can water	1 can French-fried onion rings

Combine the soups, water and chicken in a large frypan. Stir in the rice and bring to a boil. Cover and reduce heat to medium low. Simmer for 7 minutes. Stir well, then sprinkle the onion rings on top. 6-8 servings.

Mrs. Albert Calhoun, Greeneville, Tennessee

SIMPLE CHICKEN
Preparation and cooking time about 1 hour

1 fryer, cut up	Celery salt
2 c. packaged biscuit mix	Paprika
Salt and pepper to taste	

Roll the chicken in the biscuit mix. Place in a greased shallow baking dish. Sprinkle with salt and pepper. Sprinkle a small amount of celery salt and paprika over top. Bake in 375-degree oven for 45 minutes or until chicken is golden brown.

Audrey A. Engstrom, Tampa, Florida

QUICK SKILLET DINNER
Emergency shelf ingredients; mix and cook for 30 minutes

2 tbsp. chopped onion	1 can cream of mushroom soup
1/2 c. diced celery	2 cans chicken broth
1/4 c. margarine	2 c. diced cooked chicken
1 10-oz. package noodles	1 tsp. salt
1 can cream of chicken soup	

Preheat electric skillet to 350 degrees. Saute the onion and celery in the margarine, then add remaining ingredients. Increase temperature to 400 degrees and bring to a boil, stirring constantly. Reduce temperature to 200 degrees. Simmer, covered, with vent closed for 15 minutes or until noodles are tender. 8 servings.

Carolyn Wayman, Mooreland, Oklahoma

ROKA CHICKEN
Easily prepared; allow 1 hour for baking

1 fryer-broiler, cut up	Roka blue cheese dressing
Flour	Paprika
Salt and pepper to taste	

Coat the chicken with seasoned flour and dip in the dressing. Place in a baking dish and sprinkle with paprika. Bake at 350 degrees for 50 to 60 minutes.

Roka Chicken (above)

QUICK AND EASY CHICKEN PIE
Emergency shelf ingredients; mix and bake for 30 minutes

1 pkg. frozen mixed vegetables	1 sm. can chicken broth
1 can boned chicken	1 can refrigerator biscuits

Combine the mixed vegetables, chicken and broth in a large, shallow baking dish and top with biscuits. Bake at 350 degrees for 30 minutes or until biscuits are brown. 6 servings.

Mrs. Inez Richards, Silver Spring, Maryland

JIFFY CHICKEN CHOW MEIN
Quick leftovers dividend; 30 minutes cooking time

2 c. diced cooked chicken	1 can cream of chicken soup
1 1-lb. can chow mein vegetables, drained	1 can cream of mushroom soup
1 3-lb. can chow mein noodles	1 c. milk
	1 to 3 tsp. soy sauce

Combine the chicken, vegetables and noodles. Combine remaining ingredients. Add to the chicken mixture and mix well. Turn into a greased 1 1/2-quart baking dish. Bake at 350 degrees for 30 minutes. 6 servings.

Mrs. William Strieber, Crofton, Maryland

SWEET AND SOUR CHICKEN
Fancy, yet easy to prepare; allow 1 hour and 30 minutes for baking

3 lb. chicken parts	1 env. onion soup mix
8 oz. Russian dressing	10 oz. apricot preserves

Arrange the chicken in a baking dish. Mix the dressing, onion soup mix and preserves and pour over the chicken. Bake for 1 hour and 30 minutes at 350 degrees. Baste occasionally. 6 servings.

Mrs. Philip Renner, Enterprise, Alabama

FAVORITE CHICKEN PIE
Partially prepared ahead; allow 45 minutes for cooking

1 sm. hen	1 sm. onion, chopped
1 can cream of chicken soup	1/2 c. chopped celery
1 soup can water	1 recipe biscuit dough
1 can mixed vegetables	

Cook the hen in boiling, salted water until tender. Remove from broth and cool. Remove chicken from bones and cut in large pieces. Add the soup, water, mixed vegetables, onion and celery and mix well. Place in a large baking dish. Roll out the biscuit dough on a floured surface to size of baking dish and place over chicken mixture. Bake at 350 degrees for 45 minutes.

Mrs. Mable Shaffeur, Maynardville, Tennessee

VIVA LA CHICKEN
Easily prepared in 15 minutes; allow 1 hour for baking

1 pkg. corn tortillas	2 cans cream of chicken soup
6 c. chopped cooked chicken	1 soup can milk
1 lb. extra sharp cheese, grated	1 7-oz. jar chilies, chopped

Grease a 3-quart casserole. Cut the tortillas in 1-inch strips and arrange in layers in the casserole alternating with chicken and cheese. Combine the soup, milk and chilies and pour over the top layer. Mix lightly, then cover. Bake for 45 minutes at 300 degrees. Uncover and bake for 15 minutes longer.

Mrs. Thomas D. Farrell, Biloxi, Mississippi

BONELESS TURKEY ROLL
Easily prepared; allow 4 hours for baking

1 7-lb. frozen turkey roll	Tasty Basting Sauce
Barbecue salt to taste	

Thaw the turkey roll in the original bag in the refrigerator. Remove the bag and leave the string or net in place. Sprinkle generously with barbecue salt and place the roast on a rack in a shallow baking pan. Bake at 325 degrees, basting with Tasty Basting Sauce frequently, for about 3 hours and 30 minutes or until meat thermometer registers 175 degrees. Cover loosely with foil, if necessary, to prevent the turkey from becoming too brown during baking. Allow to stand 20 to 30 minutes before slicing.

Tasty Basting Sauce

1/2 c. salad oil	1/2 tsp. paprika
2 tbsp. chopped onion	1/2 tsp. pepper
1 garlic clove, minced	1/4 tsp. dry mustard
1 tsp. sugar	2 tbsp. vinegar
1 tsp. salt	1 tsp. Worcestershire sauce

Combine all the sauce ingredients in a small saucepan and simmer for 30 minutes. Store in a covered jar in the refrigerator to use for basting turkey.

Photograph for this recipe on page 4.

TURKEY CROQUETTES
Partially prepared ahead; allow 20 minutes for cooking

1 c. thick white sauce	1 tsp. poultry seasoning
1/2 tsp. salt	Spices to taste
1/4 tsp. pepper	Sifted crumbs
2 c. ground cooked turkey meat	1 egg, beaten

Combine all the ingredients except the crumbs and egg. Spread on a plate and chill. Shape 1 rounded tablespoon of mixture for each croquette. Roll in crumbs, then egg and again in crumbs. Fry in 375-degree fat. 6-7 servings.

Mrs. Wayne Knox, Birmingham, Alabama

HOLIDAY EASE
Quick leftovers dividend; 20 minutes baking time

1 10 1/2-oz. package frozen peas
2 c. diced cooked turkey
1 1/2 c. cooked noodles
2 tbsp. butter
1/4 c. chopped onion
1 2-oz. can mushrooms, drained
1 can cream of mushroom soup
1/2 c. milk
1/2 tsp. monosodium glutamate
1/4 tsp. curry powder
1/2 tsp. poultry seasoning
1 c. shredded Cheddar cheese

Separate the peas under cold, running water and drain. Stir in the turkey and noodles and place in a greased 2-quart casserole. Melt the butter in a saucepan. Add the onion and mushrooms and cook until tender. Blend in soup, milk and seasonings and pour over turkey mixture. Top with the cheese. Bake in a 350-degree oven for about 20 minutes.

Barbara Berry, Vernon, Texas

EASY AND DELICIOUS TURKEY
20 minutes to prepare; 20 minutes to cook

1 c. milk
1 egg
1 tbsp. liquid shortening
1 c. pancake mix
1/8 tsp. thyme
1 sm. onion, grated
1/2 c. diced cooked turkey
Hot cranberry sauce

Place the milk, egg and shortening in a shaker or glass jar. Add the pancake mix, thyme and onion. Shake vigorously 10 to 15 times or until batter is fairly smooth. Pour about 1/4 cup batter for each pancake onto hot, lightly greased griddle. Sprinkle with diced turkey before turning. Bake to a golden brown, turning only once. Stack 2 pancakes together, spooning cranberry sauce between and over the pancakes. 4 servings.

Mrs. L. O. Freeman, Houston, Mississippi

TURKEY WITH ORANGE RICE
Preparation and cooking time less than 1 hour

2 tbsp. butter or margarine
2 tbsp. flour
1 c. milk
1/2 c. orange juice
1 c. sour cream
1 tbsp. parsley flakes
2 c. cooked rice
2 peeled oranges, sliced
4 c. chopped cooked turkey
1/2 c. slivered almonds

Melt the butter in a medium saucepan. Stir in the flour and cook until smooth. Add the milk, small amount at a time and cook until smooth and thickened. Do not boil. Add the orange juice and sour cream and remove from heat. Mix the parsley with rice and place in 6-cup casserole. Cover with half the orange slices. Add the turkey and pour sauce over turkey. Add remaining orange slices and sprinkle with almonds. Bake at 350 degrees for 25 to 30 minutes. 6 servings.

Mrs. Joe Shelby, Vicksburg, Mississippi

AFTER HOLIDAY TURKEY DISH
Quick leftovers dividend; 30 minutes baking time

2 c. cubed baked turkey	1 tsp. salt
2 1/2 c. turkey broth	1/2 tsp. pepper
1 pkg. noodle soup mix	1/4 tsp. basil
1 sm. can slant-cut green beans	1 c. packaged precooked rice

Combine the turkey, broth, soup mix, beans, seasonings and rice in a baking dish and let stand for 10 minutes. Cover the baking dish with lid or foil. Bake at 375 degrees for 30 minutes. 4-6 servings.

Beatrice Benton, Columbus, Georgia

QUICK TURKEY CURRY
Quick leftovers dividend; 15 minutes cooking time

1 tsp. salt	1/4 c. flour
1 10-oz. package frozen	Dash of pepper
cut asparagus	1 2/3 c. evaporated milk
2 tbsp. butter	2 c. cubed cooked turkey
1 tsp. curry powder	6 slices toast

Cook the salt and asparagus in 1/4 cup water for 5 to 6 minutes or until the asparagus is almost tender. Remove from heat. Add the butter and stir until melted. Blend in curry powder, flour and pepper, a small amount at a time, stirring to mix smoothly. Stir in the evaporated milk and 1/3 cup water, keeping mixture smooth. Add the turkey and cook over low heat, stirring frequently, until sauce is thickened and smooth. Serve over hot toast. 5-6 servings.

Quick Turkey Curry (above)

seafood

Seafood almost seems to have been made especially for quick and easy cookery — most varieties take just minutes to cook. Seafood is versatile — and this versatility combined with short cooking times have led southern homemakers to develop many timesaving recipes using all types of fish and shellfish.

Now the best of these recipes are featured in the pages which follow, recipes certain to bring praise from family and friends — and good eating for all. What could be easier, for instance, than a Do-ahead Crab Souffle — or more perfectly elegant for a luncheon or late-evening supper. And treat your family to one of the South's proudest dishes — Maryland Crab Cakes. This traditional shellfish recipe has been updated for twentieth century homemakers who want to prepare great foods without spending all day in their kitchens.

Treat everyone to the mild and delicious flavor of fish and feature Batter-fried Fish Fillets. Batter-frying is a southern way of preparing fish that ensures flavor and texture contrast — and helps protect the delicate flesh of fish as well! Salmon Croquettes... Tuna-Cheese Puffs ... Tuna with Celery Sauce are three more recipes you'll find in these pages.

All recipes in this section have been favorites with families throughout the Southland for years. Now they're waiting to become favorites in your home, too!

CREAMED CRAB MEAT OVER MUFFINS
Elegant, yet easy to prepare; 20 minutes to cook

1/3 c. chopped green pepper	1/8 tsp. thyme
Butter	1/4 tsp. Worcestershire sauce
1 can mushroom soup	2 cans crab meat, drained
1 can evaporated milk	and boned
1 tsp. salt	1/4 c. chopped pimento
1/4 tsp. marjoram	6 English muffins, split
1/4 tsp. dry mustard	

Saute the green pepper in 2 tablespoons butter until tender-crisp. Blend in the soup and milk gradually, then stir in salt, marjoram, mustard, thyme, Worcestershire sauce, crab meat and pimento. Heat thoroughly. Toast the muffins until brown and spread with butter. Serve the creamed crab meat over the muffins.

Mrs. Henry McDaniel, Oklahoma City, Oklahoma

EASY CLUB LUNCHEON

Creamed Crab Meat over Muffins *page 84*
Broccoli with Lemon Butter *page 102*
Apricot Pie *page 169*

DO-AHEAD CRAB SOUFFLE
Prepare ahead and refrigerate; allow 1 hour and 15 minutes to bake

8 slices bread	4 eggs, slightly beaten
1/2 c. mayonnaise	3 c. milk
1 med. green pepper, chopped	1 can cream of mushroom soup
2 c. crab meat	1 c. grated sharp Cheddar
1 onion, chopped	cheese
1/2 c. chopped celery	Paprika to taste

Dice 4 slices bread and place in a greased 9 x 13-inch baking dish. Mix the mayonnaise, green pepper, crab meat, onion and celery and spread over bread. Trim crusts from remaining bread and place over crab mixture. Blend the eggs and milk and pour over casserole. Refrigerate overnight. Bake at 325 degrees for 15 minutes. Spread soup over bread, then sprinkle with cheese and paprika. Bake for 1 hour longer. 12 servings.

Mrs. J. H. Patterson, Bay City, Texas

ELEGANT CRAB PIE
Partially prepared ahead; place in oven 20 minutes before serving time

2 6-oz. packages frozen	1 tsp. paprika
crab meat	1/2 c. chopped green pepper
2 c. finely crushed corn chips	1/2 c. finely chopped onion
6 tbsp. melted margarine or	3 tbsp. flour
butter	1 tsp. salt

| 1/4 tsp. pepper | 1 c. sour cream |
| 1/2 c. milk | 1/2 c. sliced stuffed olives |

Thaw the crab meat and flake. Combine the corn chips, 2 tablespoons margarine and paprika and reserve 1/3 cup. Press remaining corn chip mixture on bottom and side of 9-inch shallow casserole. Bake at 375 degrees for 10 minutes, then cool. Cook the green pepper and onion in remaining margarine in a saucepan until soft. Blend in the flour, salt and pepper. Add the milk and sour cream and cook over low heat, stirring constantly, until thickened. Stir in the olives and crab meat and spoon into crust. Sprinkle with reserved corn chip mixture. Bake at 350 degrees for 15 minutes and serve hot. 4-6 servings.

Mrs. Frances A. Dickey, Sadler, Texas

MARYLAND CRAB CAKES
20 minutes to prepare; 20 minutes to cook

1 sm. onion, chopped	1 lb. crab meat
2 tbsp. diced celery	1/2 tsp. salt
1 med. green pepper, chopped	1/2 tsp. red pepper
1 tbsp. butter	1/2 tsp. thyme
1 1/2 c. bread crumbs	2 tbsp. mayonnaise
1 egg, beaten	

Brown the onion, celery and green pepper lightly in butter. Mix the bread crumbs and egg well, then add the vegetables. Stir in the crab meat and add salt, red pepper, thyme and mayonnaise. Mix well. Shape into cakes and fry in small amount of fat in a skillet until golden brown. 6 servings.

Genevieve A. Mitchell, La Plata, Maryland

CREAMED LOBSTER AND MACARONI
Prepared and cooked in 1 hour

2 c. chopped lobster	2 1/2 tsp. paprika
Butter	3 1/2 c. milk
1/3 c. flour	1/3 c. sherry
2 tsp. salt	8 oz. elbow macaroni
1/4 tsp. pepper	1/2 c. grated Parmesan cheese

Saute the lobster in 1/4 cup butter. Melt 1/3 cup butter in a large saucepan and blend in the flour, salt, pepper and paprika. Add the milk gradually and cook, stirring constantly until thickened. Add the lobster and sherry. Cook macaroni in boiling salted water until tender and drain. Add the macaroni to the lobster mixture. Turn into a lightly greased 2-quart casserole and sprinkle with Parmesan cheese. Pour 1/4 cup melted butter over cheese. Bake in 350-degree oven for 20 to 25 minutes or until sauce is bubbly and cheese is melted and delicately brown. 4-6 servings.

Mrs. Andrew Young, Panama City, Florida

South African Fry (below)

SOUTH AFRICAN FRY
Elegant but quickly prepared; less than 5 minutes to fry

3 8-oz. packages South African rock lobster-tails	6 tbsp. (about) fine bread crumbs
1 egg, lightly beaten	1 lb. vegetable shortening

Parboil the frozen South African rock lobster-tails by dropping into boiling salted water. Bring to a boil again, then drain immediately and drench with cold water. Cut away underside membrane by snipping along each edge with shears and stripping off. Remove meat carefully from shell in one piece. Roll whole rock lobster-tails in egg and then lightly in bread crumbs. Melt the shortening in a deep pan and heat over low heat until a wisp of smoke or steam rises. Lower the breaded lobster-tails gently into the hot fat in a basket or with a slotted spoon and cook for 2 to 3 minutes until golden brown. Remove the lobster-tails and drain on absorbent paper and serve immediately with tartar sauce. 6 servings.

LOBSTER NEWBURG
Fancy, yet easy to prepare; allow 30 minutes for cooking

1/3 c. butter or margarine	1/4 c. sherry
2 tbsp. flour	2 tsp. lemon juice
2 c. light cream	1/2 tsp. salt
3 egg yolks, beaten	Dash of paprika
3 c. cooked or canned lobster	6 frozen patty shells, baked
1 4-oz. can button mushrooms	

Melt the butter in a chafing dish or skillet and blend in the flour. Stir in the cream and cook over low heat until sauce thickens, stirring constantly. Place hot water in the bottom part of the chafing dish. Stir a small amount of hot mixture into the egg yolks and return to the hot mixture. Cook until thick, stirring constantly. Add the lobster, mushrooms, sherry, lemon juice, and salt and sprinkle with paprika. Spoon into warm baked patty shells to serve.

Mrs. Donald Ball, Newport News, Virginia

BAKED CREAMED OYSTERS
Quickly prepared; 20 minutes cooking time

25 med. oysters and liquid	3 1/2 tbsp. butter
1 tsp. salt	2 tbsp. flour
1/8 tsp. pepper	1/2 c. milk
1/8 tsp. nutmeg	1/2 c. cream
1/2 tsp. minced parsley	1/2 c. buttered cracker
1/2 tsp. onion juice	crumbs

Cook the oysters in oyster liquid in a saucepan for 5 minutes. Drain and chop. Add the salt, pepper, nutmeg, parsley and onion juice and place in a baking dish. Melt butter in the saucepan and stir in the flour. Add milk gradually and cook for 2 minutes or until thickened. Add cream and remove from heat. Stir into oyster mixture in baking dish and cover with the crumbs. Bake at 375 degrees until brown. 6 servings.

Mrs. James E. Griffith, Boyle, Mississippi

SAUCY OYSTERS
Easily prepared and cooked in about 30 minutes

1 qt. small or cut oysters	1 c. catsup
Butter	3 tbsp. Worcestershire sauce
2 tbsp. flour	1/4 tsp. hot sauce

Drain and reserve the oyster liquid, then add water, if needed, to make 1 cup liquid. Melt 2 tablespoons butter in a saucepan and blend in the flour. Add the oyster liquid and cook, stirring constantly, until thick. Add the catsup and sauces and bring to a boil. Add the oysters and bring again to a boil. Add about 2 tablespoons butter and serve over toast. 8 servings.

Mrs. Rogers Webb, Cascade, Maryland

SCALLOPED OYSTERS
Preparation and cooking time less than 1 hour

2 sticks butter	2 cans oysters, drained
1 c. bread crumbs	6 tbsp. cream
1 1/2 c. cracker crumbs	Salt and pepper to taste

Melt the butter and mix with the bread and cracker crumbs. Combine the oysters, cream, salt and pepper. Arrange layers of the oyster mixture and crumb mixture, ending with crumbs on top, in a baking dish. Bake for 30 minutes at 350 degrees. 6 servings.

Mrs. Merritt Kent, Selbyville, Delaware

SHRIMP AND DEVILED EGGS
Preparation and cooking time less than 1 hour

8 deviled eggs	1 tbsp. chopped parsley
2 lb. cooked shrimp	1 tbsp. Worcestershire sauce
2 cans mushroom soup	1 tsp. salt
1/2 c. grated sharp Cheddar	1 tsp. dry mustard
cheese	1/2 c. dry sherry
Minced garlic to taste	1 c. buttered crumbs
1 tbsp. catsup	2 cans chow mein noodles

Place the eggs in a greased shallow casserole and add the shrimp. Mix remaining ingredients except crumbs and noodles in a saucepan and heat through. Pour over the shrimp and top with buttered crumbs. Bake in 350-degree oven for 30 minutes. Serve over chow mein noodles.

Mrs. Marion H. Buchanan, Lake Wales, Florida

SHRIMP AND MUSHROOMS
20 minutes to prepare; 20 minutes to bake

1 1/2 tbsp. butter or	1/4 tsp. paprika
margarine	1/2 tsp. salt
2 tbsp. chopped onion	1/2 c. grated cheese
2 tsp. chopped green pepper	1 6-oz. can mushrooms
2 tbsp. flour	1 lb. boiled shrimp, cleaned
3/4 c. half and half	1 c. buttered bread crumbs

Melt the butter in a saucepan. Add the onion and green pepper and cook until tender. Blend in the flour. Add the half and half and cook, stirring, until thickened. Add remaining ingredients except bread crumbs and pour into a buttered casserole. Top with bread crumbs. Bake at 350 degrees for 20 minutes. 4 servings.

Mrs. Ray DeLoney, Sebring, Florida

WILD RICE AND SHRIMP
Partially prepared ahead; allow 20 minutes to heat

3 c. wild rice	3 tbsp. light cream
1/2 c. butter	Salt and pepper to taste
1/4 c. minced onion	Dash of hot sauce
1/2 c. minced celery	Curry powder and sage
1 lb. small shrimp	to taste

Cook the wild rice according to package directions and drain. Add 1/4 cup butter and toss until well mixed. Pour into a casserole. Saute the onion and celery in remaining butter in a saucepan until tender and add shrimp. Add the cream and seasonings and pour over rice. Bake at 300 degrees until heated through. 12 servings.

Mrs. Frances Faircloth, Ft. Jackson, South Carolina

Angostura Barbecued Shrimp (below)

ANGOSTURA BARBECUED SHRIMP
Elegant but quickly prepared; allow 5 minutes to heat before serving

2 lb. jumbo shrimp, cooked
1/4 c. butter or margarine
1 sm. onion, minced
1 c. chili sauce

1 c. tomato juice
1 tbsp. angostura aromatic
  bitters
Juice of 1 lemon

Shell and devein the shrimp, leaving the fantail intact. Chill the shrimp until ready to cook in the sauce. Heat the butter in a large skillet and saute the onion until golden. Add the remaining ingredients and simmer until the sauce bubbles. Add the shrimp and cook for about 5 minutes until heated through. Serve on rice. 6 servings.

BAKED SEAFOOD SALAD
Quickly prepared; 45 minutes cooking time

2 c. cooked shrimp
2 c. crab meat
2 c. chopped green pepper
1/2 c. minced onion
2 c. mayonnaise

1 tbsp. Worcestershire sauce
Salt to taste
1/2 tsp. pepper
2 c. buttered bread crumbs

Combine all ingredients except 1 cup bread crumbs and mix well. Place in a casserole or individual shells and sprinkle remaining bread crumbs on top. Bake at 350 degrees for 45 minutes. Let stand for 5 minutes before serving.

Mrs. Joseph Higgins, New Orleans, Louisiana

COMPANY SEAFOOD
Partially prepared ahead; allow 1 hour for cooking

6 eggs	1 tsp. onion juice
3 c. milk	1 1/2 tsp. Worcestershire
3 c. soft bread cubes	sauce
2 c. grated American	2 drops of hot sauce
cheese	1 c. cooked sm. shrimp
1 tsp. salt	1 c. diced cooked lobster
1/4 tsp. pepper	1 c. crab meat
1/8 tsp. cayenne pepper	2 tbsp. melted butter
1/2 tsp. dry mustard	

Beat the eggs slightly in a bowl and add milk and bread cubes. Let set for about 10 minutes. Stir in cheese and seasonings. Saute the shrimp, lobster and crab meat lightly in butter and add to egg mixture. Pour into a large casserole and place in a pan of hot water. Bake in 350-degree oven for about 1 hour or until a knife inserted in center comes out clean. 10-12 servings.

Mrs. John L. Clark, Jr., Arlington, Virginia

LONG BEACH SEAFOOD
Prepared ahead and chilled; allow 1 hour for baking

2 cans frozen shrimp soup	1/2 lb. flaked crab meat
2 tbsp. sherry	1/2 lb. small cooked shrimp
1 2 1/2-oz. package slivered	Sliced American cheese
almonds	Paprika
2 sm. cans button mushrooms	

Thaw the soup according to can directions, but do not dilute. Place in a 2-quart casserole and stir in the sherry and almonds. Drain the mushrooms and add to soup mixture. Fold in the crab meat and shrimp. Cover with a layer of cheese and sprinkle with paprika. Refrigerate until chilled. Bake at 300 degrees for 1 hour and serve over rice.

Dorothy Burritt, Sarasota, Florida

QUICK SEAFOOD BAKE
Preparation and cooking time less than 1 hour

1 green pepper, diced	1/2 tsp. salt
1 onion, diced	1/8 tsp. pepper
1 c. diced celery	1 c. mayonnaise
3 c. crab meat	1 tsp. Worcestershire sauce
1/2 lb. cooked shrimp	1 c. buttered cracker crumbs

Mix all ingredients except cracker crumbs and place in a baking dish. Sprinkle crumbs on top. Bake at 350 degrees for 30 minutes or until brown.

Mrs. Betty Smith, Jesup, Georgia

BATTER-FRIED FISH FILLETS
Preparation and cooking time less than 1 hour

1 c. sifted flour	1/2 c. water
1 tsp. salt	1 egg, well beaten
1 1/2 tsp. baking powder	2 lb. fish fillets
1 1/2 tsp. monosodium glutamate	

Sift the flour, salt, baking powder and monosodium glutamate together, then add water and egg, adding more water if batter is too thick. Beat until smooth. Dip the fillets into batter. Heat deep fat to 375 degrees and fry fish until brown. 6 servings.

Martha Gambrell, Little Rock, Arkansas

BAKED HADDOCK FILLETS
Preparation and cooking time less than 1 hour

2 lb. haddock fillets	2 tbsp. flour
1/4 tsp. salt	1 tbsp. dry mustard
Dash of pepper	1 c. milk
1/4 tsp. paprika	1/2 c. bread crumbs
Juice of 1 lemon	1 tbsp. minced parsley
2 tbsp. butter	

Cut the haddock into serving pieces and place in a greased shallow pan or baking dish. Sprinkle with salt, pepper, paprika and lemon juice. Melt the butter in a saucepan and blend in the flour and dry mustard. Stir in the milk and cook, stirring constantly, until thickened. Season to taste and pour over the fillets. Sprinkle with the bread crumbs and parsley. Bake in 350-degree oven for 35 minutes. 6 servings.

Mrs. Marcia Cole, Nashville, Tennessee

FLOUNDER MEAL-IN-ONE
20 minutes to prepare; 20 minutes to bake

1/2 lb. frozen flounder fillets	Dash of pepper
3 tbsp. butter	1 1/2 c. cooked rice
1 can mushroom soup	1 10-oz. box frozen peas,
1 1/4 c. milk	thawed
1/4 c. finely chopped onion	1/2 c. grated Cheddar cheese
1/4 tsp. salt	Dash of paprika

Saute the fillets in butter and cut in cubes. Combine the soup, milk, onion, salt and pepper in a saucepan and bring to a boil, stirring occasionally. Add the rice, flounder and peas. Place in a casserole. Top with the cheese and sprinkle with paprika. Bake, covered, for 20 minutes at 375 degrees. 4 servings.

Mrs. M. Huff, Blytheville, Arkansas

Baked Halibut Surprise (below)

BAKED HALIBUT SURPRISE
Allow 30 minutes for marinating; prepared and cooked in 30 minutes

2 lb. halibut steaks, fresh
  or frozen
1/2 c. French dressing
2 tbsp. lemon juice
1/4 tsp. salt

1 3 1/2-oz. can French-
  fried onions
1/4 c. grated Parmesan
  cheese

Thaw frozen steaks and cut into serving-size portions. Place the halibut in a shallow baking dish. Combine the dressing, lemon juice and salt and pour over the halibut. Let stand for 30 minutes, turning once. Remove the halibut from the sauce and place in a well-greased baking dish. Crush the onions, then add the cheese and mix thoroughly. Sprinkle the onion mixture over the halibut. Bake at 350 degrees for 25 to 30 minutes or until fish flakes easily when tested with a fork. 6 servings.

SAUCY PORTIONS
Quickly prepared; 30 minutes cooking time

6 frozen 3-oz. breaded fish
  portions
2 tbsp. melted fat or oil
Paprika
1 14 1/2-oz. can green
  asparagus spears

1 10-oz. can frozen cream
  of shrimp soup
1/3 c. milk
1/4 c. grated sharp cheese
1 tbsp. horseradish
Paprika

Place the frozen fish on a well-greased baking sheet and drizzle fat over the fish. Sprinkle with paprika. Bake at 500 degrees for 15 to 20 minutes or until fish is brown and flakes easily when tested with a fork. Bring the asparagus to a boil and drain. Combine the soup and milk and heat until the soup is thawed, stirring occasionally. Add the cheese and horseradish and blend thoroughly. Arrange the asparagus on fish portions. Pour the sauce over the asparagus and sprinkle with paprika. 6 servings.

Photograph for this recipe on page 82.

DELUXE BAKED RED SNAPPER
Easily prepared; allow 45 minutes for baking

1 red snapper	3 slices of bacon
Salt and pepper to taste	2 to 3 c. grapefruit juice

Place the red snapper in a baking pan and season with salt and pepper. Lay the bacon over the snapper and add juice to half cover fish. Bake in 350-degree oven for about 45 minutes or until done. Serve on heated platter.

Mrs. Mimi Bice, Winter Haven, Florida

SIMPLE SALMON DINNER

Salmon Croquettes *page 93*
Tiny English Peas and Mushrooms in Butter *page 114*
Crescent Rolls *page 182*
Orange Flambe *page 162*

SALMON CROQUETTES
Emergency shelf ingredients; mix and cook in 20 minutes

2 c. fine cracker crumbs	Juice of 1 lemon
1 7 3/4-oz. can pink salmon	2 tbsp. Worcestershire sauce
1 egg	1/3 c. catsup
Salt and pepper to taste	1 egg white, slightly beaten

Combine 1 cup cracker crumbs with all remaining ingredients except egg white. Shape the salmon mixture into patties. Dip the patties into egg white, then roll in remaining cracker crumbs. Fry in hot deep fat until brown.

Mrs. Sue Batchelor, Gordo, Alabama

SAVORY SALMON LOAF
Quickly prepared; 45 minutes cooking time

1 1-lb. can salmon	2 eggs, slightly beaten
1 1/2 c. stuffing mix	1 can cream of mushroom soup
1/4 c. minced onion	

Combine the salmon, stuffing mix, onion, eggs and soup and pack into a greased loaf pan. Bake in 350-degree oven for 45 to 50 minutes or until center is firm. Remove from oven and let stand for 5 minutes in pan. Turn out onto a heated serving platter and serve with tomato or cheese sauce, if desired. 4-6 servings.

Mrs. John K. Wright, Key West, Florida

RED SNAPPER WITH CORN BREAD STUFFING
Preparation and cooking time about 1 hour and 30 minutes

1 3 to 4-lb. red snapper	Salt and pepper to taste
2 c. cornmeal	2 eggs, beaten
Butter	3 slices salt pork
3 med. onions, chopped	

Place the snapper in a shallow baking pan. Combine the cornmeal, 1/2 cup melted butter, onions, salt, pepper and eggs in a bowl and mix well. Stuff the cornmeal mixture into the snapper and place the salt pork over the top, then cover. Bake at 375 degrees for 1 hour, then uncover and bake until brown. The snapper may be wrapped in foil, if desired.

Photograph for this recipe on page 2.

TROPHY TROUT
Allow 1 hour for marinating; prepared and cooked in 10 minutes

3 lb. pan-dressed rainbow trout	1 pkg. onion soup mix
1 c. buttermilk	1 c. flour
	Lemon wedges

Clean, wash and dry the trout and place in a single layer in a shallow baking dish. Combine the buttermilk and soup mix and brush fish inside and out. Let stand for 1 hour. Remove the trout from the sauce and roll in flour. Fry the fish in hot fat over moderate heat for 4 to 5 minutes or until brown. Turn carefully and fry for 4 to 5 minutes longer or until brown and fish flakes easily when tested with a fork. Drain on absorbent paper. Serve with lemon wedges. 6 servings.

Trophy Trout (above)

TROUT FILLET DELUXE
Partially prepared ahead; allow 50 minutes for baking

6 fillets of trout
4 slices bacon
1 c. grated carrots
2 tbsp. chopped celery
1 c. chopped onions
1 c. chopped mushrooms
2 tbsp. minced parsley

1/2 tsp. thyme
2 tsp. salt
1/2 tsp. pepper
1/2 c. diced ham
1 c. white wine
3 tbsp. butter or margarine

Preheat oven to 375 degrees. Cut the fillets in half. Cook the bacon until partially done and drain. Place in a casserole. Mix the carrots, celery, onions, mushrooms, parsley, thyme, salt, pepper and ham and spread half the mixture over bacon. Arrange fish fillets over vegetable mixture and cover with remaining vegetable mixture. Pour wine over all and dot with butter. Bake for 50 minutes. 6 servings.

Mrs. John H. Kolek, Lakeland, Florida

SOLE SUPREME
20 minutes to prepare; 20 minutes to bake

6 fillets of sole
1 c. chopped green peppers
4 sm. green onions, chopped
16 mushrooms, sliced
Pinch of rosemary (opt.)
1/4 tsp. Beau Monde seasoning

Salt and pepper to taste
1/4 c. butter
Juice of 1 lemon
1/2 c. light cream
1 c. dry white wine
6 tbsp. slivered almonds

Place fillets in a greased 7 x 12-inch casserole. Saute the green peppers, onions, mushrooms, rosemary, Beau Monde seasoning, salt and pepper in butter in a saucepan until onions are tender. Add the lemon juice, cream and wine. Bring to boiling point and pour over fillets. Sprinkle with almonds. Bake in 350-degree oven for 20 minutes. May be refrigerated before baking. 6 servings.

Mrs. Howard Robinson, Danville, Virginia

TUNA AND CHIPS
Preparation and cooking time less than 1 hour

2 cans cream of mushroom soup
2 c. noodles, cooked and
   drained
2 cans tuna
1/2 c. grated Cheddar cheese

1 sm. jar olives, sliced
1/4 lb. cashew nuts, chopped
1/2 c. milk
Potato chips, crushed
Paprika

Pour 1 can of mushroom soup in a buttered casserole. Add the noodles, tuna, cheese, olives and nuts. Top with remaining soup and milk and stir gently. Top with potato chips and sprinkle with paprika. Bake at 350 degrees until bubbly and golden brown on top. 6-8 servings.

Mrs. Nancy W. Grammer, Ripley, Tennessee

SWEET AND SOUR TUNA
Emergency shelf ingredients; mix and cook for 30 minutes

1 lge. can pineapple chunks	2 tbsp. vinegar
2 tbsp. butter or margarine	6 tbsp. sugar
2 c. green pepper strips	Salt to taste
1 c. water	1/8 tsp. pepper
1 chicken bouillon cube	2 7-oz. cans tuna
2 tbsp. cornstarch	Chow mein noodles
1 tbsp. soy sauce	

Drain the pineapple, reserving liquid. Cook the pineapple chunks in butter for 3 minutes. Add 3/4 cup reserved liquid and simmer for 5 minutes. Add the green pepper and simmer for 5 minutes longer. Add water and bouillon cube and bring to a boil. Mix remaining reserved liquid with cornstarch and add to pineapple mixture, stirring constantly. Add the soy sauce, vinegar, sugar and seasonings and cook, stirring constantly, until thickened. Fold in the tuna and heat to serving temperature. Serve over warm noodles. 4 servings.

Mrs. Judy Wood, Newark, Delaware

TUNA-CHEESE PUFFS
Partially prepared ahead; allow 50 minutes for cooking

8 slices firm white bread	1/8 tsp. pepper
1 7-oz. can tuna, drained	1/2 tsp. paprika
4 slices Cheddar cheese	1 tbsp. parsley flakes
2 tbsp. butter	2 eggs, slightly beaten
1/2 tsp. dry mustard	1 c. milk
1/4 tsp. salt	

Preheat oven to 350 degrees. Remove the crust from the bread and place half the bread in a shallow 1 1/2-quart casserole. Flake the tuna and sprinkle over the bread. Cover with the cheese. Butter both sides of remaining bread and place over the cheese. Combine remaining ingredients and pour over the bread. Let stand for 15 minutes. Bake for 50 minutes. Cut into squares. 4 servings.

Mrs. A. C. Gilmer, Fort Smith, Arkansas

TUNA WITH CELERY SAUCE
Emergency shelf ingredients; mix and cook for 30 minutes

1 can tuna	Chopped onion and green
1 can French-style green beans	pepper (opt.)
1 can cream of celery soup	Buttered bread crumbs

Place all ingredients except crumbs in alternating layers in a greased baking dish. Cover with buttered bread crumbs. Bake for 30 minutes at 375 degrees. 4-6 servings.

Jean C. Vandergrift, Roanoke, Virginia

TUNA TUMBLE
Emergency shelf ingredients; mix and cook for 20 minutes

1 1/3 c. instant rice	1 c. cooked peas, drained
1/4 c. chopped onion	1/2 c. Cheddar cheese soup
1/4 c. chopped green pepper	1/4 c. evaporated milk
1 tbsp. cooking oil	1 tsp. prepared mustard
1 6 1/2-oz. can tuna	

Prepare the rice according to package directions. Saute the onion and green pepper in oil in a large skillet. Add the rice, tuna and peas. Blend and heat soup in a saucepan with milk and mustard. Pour the sauce over the tuna mixture and mix lightly. Cook until heated through. 6 servings.

Mrs. Alice Johnson, Winston-Salem, North Carolina

TUNA-TOMATO COMBO
Preparation and cooking time about 30 minutes

1 c. chopped onions	1/2 tsp. salt
2 tbsp. butter or margarine	Dash of pepper
2 tbsp. flour	1/2 tsp. curry powder or
1 14 1/2-oz. can stewed	oregano
tomatoes	1 13-oz. can tuna
1/3 c. sliced stuffed olives	3 c. hot cooked rice
2 tbsp. parsley flakes	

Saute the onions in the butter until tender, then blend in the flour. Add the tomatoes, olives, parsley and seasonings. Cook, stirring constantly, until thickened. Drain and flake the tuna and stir into the tomato sauce. Serve the tuna-tomato mixture over the rice. 6 servings.

Tuna-Tomato Combo (above)

Asparagus with Orange and Cashew Cream Sauce (page 100)
Acorn Squash with Sliced Apples (page 114)

vegetables

Homemakers seeking foods which can be prepared quickly and easily delight in vegetables — nearly every one profits from short cooking time. In fact, you just cook them enough to bring them to the peak of their tender-crisp goodness — only minutes in the case of most vegetables whether frozen, canned, or garden-fresh.

Southern Living cooks have created recipes for vegetable dishes that are eagerly awaited by their hungry families. The finest of these recipes, selected particularly for their quick and easy preparation, have been included in the section that follows.

In these pages, you'll discover a recipe for Asparagus Rice Supreme, a dish that provides flavor and color contrast to harmonize with virtually every main dish. And when ham, frankfurters, or hamburgers are featured at your home, highlight them with Baked Beans Hawaiian, a zesty and unexpected blend of flavors that will bring new excitement to a quick meal.

These are recipes hundreds of southern women rely upon for flavors their families enjoy — and timesaving preparation they themselves appreciate! Every recipe has been tested and perfected by a woman like you, whose primary concern is feeding her family the foods they need. Best of all, these recipes save you time — and isn't that something we can all use!

ASPARAGUS WITH ORANGE AND CASHEW CREAM SAUCE
Elegant but quickly prepared; 20 minutes cooking time

2 1/2 lb. fresh asparagus	2 c. milk
Salt	1 fresh orange, sectioned
4 tbsp. margarine	1/2 c. chopped cashews
4 tbsp. flour	

Cook the asparagus in boiling salted water until tender and drain. Melt the margarine in a saucepan, then stir in the flour until blended. Add the milk gradually, stirring constantly. Cook and stir until sauce is smooth and thick. Cut the orange sections in large pieces and add with the cashews to the sauce. Place the asparagus in a serving dish and pour over the orange and cashew cream sauce.

Photograph for this recipe on page 98.

ASPARAGUS-RICE SUPREME
Elegant but quickly prepared; 30 minutes for cooking

1 lge. can chopped mushrooms	2 tbsp. butter
1 c. rice	2 tbsp. flour
1 No. 2 can asparagus	1/2 tsp. salt

Drain the mushrooms, reserving 1/2 cup liquid. Cook the rice according to package directions until tender and pat into an oval dish or salad mold. Invert onto a hot platter. Heat the asparagus and liquid in a saucepan and drain, reserving 1 1/2 cups liquid. Stand the asparagus around the rice for garnish. Melt the butter in a saucepan and blend in the flour and salt. Add reserved asparagus liquid gradually and cook, stirring constantly, until thickened. Add the mushrooms and mushroom liquid. Pour over the rice and asparagus. 8 servings.

Mrs. Scott Reed, Groesbeck, Texas

EASY FAMILY DINNER MENU
Beef with Horseradish *page 45*
Pickled Onion and Beet Slices *page 36*
French Beans *page 100*
Hot Sesame Bread *page 178*
Dieter's Cheesecake *page 167*

FRENCH BEANS
Emergency shelf ingredients; mix and cook for 30 minutes

2 cans French-style green beans	1 can fried onion rings
2 cans mushroom soup	

Combine the beans and soup in a baking dish. Bake in a 350-degree oven for 30 minutes. Turn the oven off and place the onion rings on top of the bean mixture. Leave in oven for 5 to 10 minutes longer. 6 servings.

Mrs. F. A. Saunders, Sr., Hampton, Virginia

WHITE BEANS IN TOMATO SAUCE
Allow 12 hours for soaking; prepared and cooked in 2 hours

1 1/2 c. dried white beans	2 tbsp. flour
1 onion, chopped	1 can tomatoes
2 tbsp. chopped green pepper	1/2 c. molasses
Butter	1/4 c. brown sugar

Soak the beans in water to cover for 12 hours, then bring to a boil and cook until tender. Saute the onion and green pepper in a small amount of butter in a saucepan until tender, then remove and set aside. Melt 2 tablespoons of butter in the saucepan and blend in the flour. Drain the tomatoes and pour the juice gradually into the flour mixture, stirring constantly. Cook and stir until thickened, then add the molasses and brown sugar. Cook, stirring constantly until the sugar is melted. Combine the beans, onion, pepper, tomatoes and sauce in a serving dish and garnish with parsley. Cooked fresh tomatoes may be used for the sauce.

Photograph for this recipe on cover.

HARICOTS VERTS A LA MAITRE D'HOTEL
20 minutes to prepare; 20 minutes to cook

1 lb. fresh green beans	1/16 tsp. ground black pepper
Salt	1 1/2 tbsp. chopped fresh
3 tbsp. butter or margarine	parsley
1/2 tsp. sugar	Cherry tomatoes

Wash and remove the tips from the beans. Cut into 1-inch pieces. Place in saucepan with 1 inch boiling water and 1 teaspoon salt. Cook, uncovered, for 5 minutes, then cover and cook for 10 to 15 minutes or only until crisp-tender. Drain, if necessary. Add the butter, sugar, 1/4 teaspoon salt, black pepper and parsley and toss lightly. Serve hot, garnished with cherry tomatoes, cut in half. 6 servings.

Haricots Verts a la Maitre D'Hotel (above)

BAKED BEANS HAWAIIAN
Emergency shelf ingredients; mix and cook for 20 minutes

1 can pork and beans	1 tbsp. Worcestershire sauce
2 tbsp. brown sugar	1 can pineapple slices
2 tbsp. onion soup mix	

Combine the pork and beans, brown sugar, soup mix and Worcestershire sauce in a baking dish. Place the pineapple slices over the bean mixture. Bake at 350 degrees until hot and bubbly. 6 servings.

Mrs. Frances Fain, Lakeland, Florida

SAVORY BEETS IN ORANGE SAUCE
Prepared and cooked in 20 minutes

6 tbsp. sugar	1 1/2 c. orange juice
3 tbsp. flour	1 tbsp. grated orange rind
1 tsp. salt	3 c. sliced cooked beets
3 c. beet liquid and water	3 tbsp. margarine

Blend the sugar, flour and salt together in a saucepan and stir in the beet liquid, orange juice and rind. Add the beets and margarine and cook over low heat until the sauce is thick and clear. 6 servings.

Mrs. David Wilson, Richmond, Virginia

BROCCOLI WITH LEMON BUTTER
Preparation and cooking time less than 30 minutes

2 10-oz. packages frozen broccoli spears	Juice of 1 lemon
3 tbsp. butter	Salt to taste

Cook the broccoli according to package directions and place in a warmed serving bowl. Melt the butter in a saucepan and add the lemon juice and salt. Stir to blend and pour over the broccoli. 8 servings.

Mrs. G. T. Lilly, Murray, Kentucky

CHEESE BROCCOLI
Quickly prepared; 1 hour baking time

1 10-oz. package frozen broccoli	1/2 c. cubed cheese
	1 can cream of mushroom soup

Place the frozen broccoli in a greased 1-quart baking dish. Add the cheese and spoon the soup over the top. Cover. Bake in 350-degree oven for 1 hour or until the broccoli is tender. 4-6 servings.

Mrs. Doris Williams, Beckley, West Virginia

STEAMED CABBAGE
Quickly prepared; less than 10 minutes cooking time

2 chicken bouillon cubes	Salt to taste
1 med. cabbage, quartered	

Dissolve the bouillon cubes in 1/2 cup boiling water. Add the cabbage and bring to a boil again. Cook for 5 minutes. Season with salt. 8 servings.

Annette Braswell, Monroe, Georgia

CABBAGE AU GRATIN
Preparation and cooking time less than 1 hour

1 med. cabbage, shredded	1/2 c. milk
2 c. diced ham	1/3 c. buttered bread crumbs
1 can cream of potato soup	

Steam the cabbage in a covered saucepan with small amount of water until slightly tender and drain. Arrange the cabbage and ham in alternate layers in a 2-quart greased casserole. Blend the soup with the milk and pour over the cabbage. Top with crumbs. Bake at 350 degrees for 30 minutes. 8 servings.

Mrs. Betty Holdorf, Wichita Falls, Texas

BAVARIAN CABBAGE
Preparation and cooking time less than 30 minutes

1 head fresh red cabbage	1 c. vinegar
1 tsp. salt	1 bay leaf
1 tbsp. bacon fat	2 whole allspice
1/2 c. sugar	

Core and slice the cabbage and place in a large saucepan. Combine the salt, bacon fat, sugar and vinegar and pour over the cabbage. Toss in the bay leaf and allspice and cover. Bring to a boil, then lower the heat and simmer until the cabbage is just tender. Remove and discard the bay leaf and allspice. Serve the cabbage with the remaining sweet and sour sauce.

Left: Braised Celery (page 106)
Right: Bavarian Cabbage (above)

103

APPLE-GLAZED CARROTS
Quick leftovers dividend; 20 minutes cooking time

1 1/2 tbsp. melted butter	1/4 c. applesauce
3 tbsp. brown sugar	2 c. cooked carrots

Combine the butter, brown sugar and applesauce in a saucepan and cook, stirring, until the brown sugar melts. Pour over the carrots in a baking dish and cover. Bake at 350 degrees for 15 minutes. 6 servings.

Mrs. Sara Royal, Rockwell, Arkansas

SAVORY CARROT STICKS
Quickly prepared; 30 minutes cooking time

6 med. carrots, scraped	1/4 tsp. thyme
6 tbsp. chopped onion	Salt and pepper to taste
3 tbsp. nonfat margarine	Minced parsley

Cut the carrots in 2-inch sticks and place in the top of a double boiler. Add the onion, margarine and thyme. Cover and cook over boiling water for 30 minutes or until crisp-tender. Season with salt and pepper. Sprinkle with minced parsley. 4 servings.

Mrs. James Shirley, Rocky Mount, North Carolina

CAULIFLOWER WITH CHEESE SAUCE
Elegant but quickly prepared; allow 30 minutes for cooking

1 med. head cauliflower	1 can cheese soup
1 tsp. salt	2 tbsp. light cream

Place the cauliflower in a saucepan and add 1 inch boiling water. Sprinkle with salt and cover. Boil for 20 minutes or until tender-crisp. Mix the soup with the cream and cook over low heat, stirring, until blended. Drain cauliflower and place on a serving platter. Top with the cheese sauce.

Letetia Davis, Goode, Virginia

CAULIFLOWER SOUFFLE
Fancy, yet easy to prepare; allow 1 hour for baking

3 tbsp. butter, melted	1 c. (heaping) chopped
3 tbsp. flour	cauliflower
1 c. milk	1 1/2 c. diced soft bread
1/2 lb. American cheese, diced	1 tsp. chopped parsley
3 eggs, beaten	Salt and pepper to taste

Blend the butter and flour in a saucepan, then add the milk gradually, stirring constantly. Cook and stir over low heat until milk mixture thickens. Add the cheese, stirring until melted. Stir a small amount of the hot cheese mixture into the eggs, then return to the saucepan. Combine the cheese sauce with the cauliflower, bread, parsley, salt and pepper and pour into a buttered ring mold. Set mold in a pan of water. Bake at 325 degrees for 1 hour. May be served with center filled with cooked peas or lima beans. 8-10 servings.

Mrs. Eloise McCoy, Miami, Florida

CAULIFLOWER DELIGHT
Emergency shelf ingredients; mix and cook for 20 minutes

2 pkg. frozen cauliflower   2 tbsp. grated Parmesan cheese
1 can cream of shrimp soup

Cook the cauliflower in a small amount of boiling water until done and drain. Melt the soup in a double boiler and pour over the cauliflower. Place in a serving dish and sprinkle with cheese.

Margaret Lindem, Ozark, Alabama

BLUE CHEESE DRESSING OVER FRESH VEGETABLES
Combine and blend in 5 minutes

1/2 c. salad oil   1/2 tsp. salt
1/4 c. finely crumbled blue   1/2 tsp. dry mustard
   cheese   1/2 tsp. paprika
3 tbsp. wine vinegar

Combine the oil, blue cheese, vinegar, salt, mustard and paprika in a bowl and beat with a mixer until well blended. Use as a marinade for cooked vegetables such as cauliflower, artichoke hearts, snap and wax beans or fresh tomatoes. Chill well before serving. About 3/4 cup.

Blue Cheese Dressing over Fresh Vegetables (above)

CHEESE-SESAME CAULIFLOWER
Quickly prepared; 20 minutes cooking time

1 med. cauliflower	1 c. shredded sharp cheese
Salt and pepper to taste	3 tsp. toasted sesame seeds
1 c. sour cream	

Separate the cauliflower into flowerets. Cover and cook in a small amount of boiling, salted water for 10 to 15 minutes or until tender and drain well. Place half the cauliflower in a 1-quart casserole. Season with salt and pepper. Spread half the sour cream over the cauliflower and sprinkle half the cheese over the sour cream. Top with half the sesame seeds and repeat the layers. Bake at 350 degrees for 5 minutes or until cheese melts and sour cream is heated through. 6 servings.

Jacqueline T. Thurmon, Castor, Louisiana

BRAISED CELERY
Preparation and cooking time about 1 hour

4 c. celery strips	1/4 c. slivered almonds
1 chicken bouillon cube	1 tbsp. cooking oil
1 onion, minced	Salt and pepper to taste
1/2 c. minced green pepper	

Cook the celery in boiling salted water for 25 minutes. Drain and reserve 1/4 cup liquid, then dissolve the bouillon cube in reserved liquid. Saute the onion and green pepper in hot oil in a heavy skillet for 10 minutes. Add the celery and bouillon and season with salt and pepper. Cover and cook over low heat for 30 minutes. Add almonds during last 10 minutes. 4 servings.

Photograph for this recipe on page 103.

CELERY AND BLEU CHEESE
20 minutes to prepare; 20 minutes to bake

4 c. coarsely sliced celery	3 tbsp. crumbled bleu cheese
1/4 c. finely chopped onion	1/2 c. heavy cream
1/4 c. chopped green pepper	1/2 tsp. salt
1 tbsp. butter	1/8 tsp. pepper
3 tbsp. cream cheese	

Cook the celery in boiling water in saucepan until tender and drain, reserving 3/4 cup broth. Saute the onion and green pepper in butter until tender, then mix in the celery broth, cream cheese, bleu cheese and cream. Stir until thoroughly blended and season with salt and pepper. Place the celery in a buttered 1 1/2-quart casserole and pour the cheese mixture over celery. Bake at 375 degrees for 20 minutes or until surface is lightly browned. 6 servings.

Mrs. Wesley Wakefield, Albany, Georgia

PARSLIED POTATOES
Preparation and cooking time less than 1 hour

1 1/2 lb. new potatoes	2 tbsp. chopped parsley
1 c. water	Dash of pepper
3/4 tsp. salt	1/4 c. flour
6 tbsp. butter	1 tall can evaporated milk

Scrape the potatoes and cut large ones in half. Place in a medium saucepan with water and salt. Cover and bring to a boil. Boil over medium heat for 20 to 25 minutes or until just tender. Add the butter, parsley and pepper. Make a paste with the flour and a small amount of cold water, then stir into the hot liquid until smooth. Add the milk and cook over low heat, stirring constantly, until the sauce is thickened. 4-6 servings.

Mrs. Marvin Ramey, Jr., Maryville, Tennessee

SUPER BAKED POTATO
Easily prepared; 45 minutes baking time

6 lge. fresh baking potatoes	Salt to taste
Margarine	

Select potatoes of uniform size and scrub thoroughly, then dry with paper towels. Rub the skins with margarine and place on a shallow baking pan. Pierce the skins with a fork several times to allow steam to escape. Bake at 400 degrees for about 45 minutes or until tender. Cut a long slit in each potato and season with salt, then top with a generous amount of margarine.

Super Baked Potato (above)

PAPRIKA POTATOES
Emergency shelf ingredients; bake for 10 minutes

2 1-lb. cans tiny whole
    potatoes, drained
1/4 c. butter

1 tsp. paprika
1 1/4 tsp. salt

Preheat oven to 425 degrees. Dry the potatoes with absorbent paper. Place the butter in a jelly roll pan and set in the oven to melt. Arrange the potatoes in melted butter, then sprinkle with paprika and salt and toss until evenly coated. Bake for 10 to 15 minutes or until heated through. Spoon into serving dish with the butter. Yield: 6 servings.

Mrs. B. C. Horrell, Nacogdoches, Texas

POTATO-CHEESE BAKE
10 minutes to prepare; 45 minutes to bake

1 lb. potatoes
1 lb. onions
1/2 lb. sharp cheese, sliced
Salt and pepper to taste

1/2 c. milk
1/2 c. bread crumbs
4 tbsp. melted butter

Pare and slice the potatoes and onions, then make alternate layers of potatoes, cheese and onions in a greased 2-quart baking dish. Sprinkle each layer with salt and pepper and pour the milk over the top layer. Sprinkle with the bread crumbs and cover with the butter. Bake at 350 degrees for 45 minutes or until potatoes are done and browned. 6 servings.

Mrs. Clara May Charlesworth, Pasadena, Maryland

SPINACH MOLD
Preparation and cooking time less than 1 hour

3 slices bacon
4 c. cooked chopped spinach
3 eggs, beaten
1/2 c. fine bread crumbs

1 8-oz. can mushrooms, sliced
1 1/2 tsp. salt
1/4 tsp. pepper

Fry the bacon until crisp, then drain and crumble. Combine the spinach, eggs, bread crumbs, bacon, mushrooms and seasonings in a greased loaf pan and set in a pan of water. Bake at 350 degrees for 45 minutes or until set. A small amount of bacon fat may be added for flavor, if desired. 8-12 servings.

Mrs. Scott K. Ross, Newport News, Virginia

SPINACH MOUSSE
Partially prepared ahead; allow 30 minutes for baking

2 pkg. frozen chopped spinach
1/4 tsp. salt
2 eggs, well beaten

1 c. evaporated milk
Dash of seasoned pepper
Dash of nutmeg

Cook the spinach with the salt according to package directions and drain well. Measure 2 cups spinach. Combine eggs, milk, pepper and nutmeg. Fold in the spinach and pour into ring mold. Place in a paper towel-lined pan and fill 2/3 full with hot water. Bake at 350 degrees for 30 minutes. 6 servings.

Katharine Rigby, Blacksburg, Virginia

SPINACH-TUNA QUADRATTINI
Preparation and cooking time about 30 minutes

1 6-oz. can broiled mushroom crowns	1/2 tsp. salt
2 10-oz. packages frozen chopped spinach, cooked	1/4 tsp. dry basil leaves
	1/2 tsp. hot sauce
2 6 1/2 or 7-oz. cans tuna in vegetable oil	1 15-oz. can tomato sauce
1 garlic clove	1 8-oz. package broad noodles, cooked
1 bay leaf	1/2 c. grated Parmesan cheese

Drain the mushrooms, reserving the liquid and several crowns for garnish. Reserve a portion of the spinach, if desired. Drain the vegetable oil from tuna into a skillet, reserving the tuna. Add the garlic, mushroom crowns, bay leaf, salt, basil and hot sauce. Saute for about 10 minutes. Add the reserved mushroom liquid, tomato sauce and tuna. Alternate layers of noodles, spinach and tuna in the sauce in an 8-cup casserole. Sprinkle the casserole with Parmesan cheese. Bake at 400 degrees for about 20 minutes. Garnish with reserved spinach and mushrooms. 6 servings.

Spinach-Tuna Quadrattini (above)

SCALLOPED CORN
Quickly prepared; allow 30 minutes for baking

2 c. cooked whole kernel corn, drained	**3/4 c. cracker crumbs**
2 eggs, well beaten	**2 tbsp. butter**
1/2 tsp. salt	**1 c. milk**

Combine the corn, eggs and salt. Place alternate layers of the corn mixture and crumbs in a greased baking dish. Dot each layer with butter. Pour the milk over the crumbs. Bake in a 325-degree oven for about 30 minutes. 6-8 servings.

Ethel Spradling, Bixby, Oklahoma

SPANISH CORN
Preparation and cooking less than 30 minutes

1/2 green pepper, chopped	**1 tsp. salt**
1 tbsp. butter	**1/4 tsp. paprika**
2 c. canned corn	**Dash of pepper**
2 tbsp. milk	**1 pimento**

Saute the green pepper in butter until just tender. Add remaining ingredients and cover. Cook slowly, stirring occasionally to prevent sticking, until corn is done. 4-5 servings.

Mrs. Winston Harris, Wilburton, Oklahoma

CUCUMBERS IN SOUR CREAM
Prepare ahead; chill until serving time

3 cucumbers	**3 tbsp. chopped chives**
1 c. sour cream	**1 1/2 tsp. salt**
2 tbsp. lemon juice	**Dash of freshly ground pepper**
2 tbsp. minced parsley	

Pare the cucumbers and cut in thin slices. Combine the sour cream, lemon juice, parsley, chives, salt and pepper and pour over the cucumbers. Chill for at least 2 hours. 4-6 servings.

Mrs. Vernon Yeager, Beaufort, South Carolina

EGGPLANT FRITTERS
Allow several hours to marinate; mix and cook in 20 minutes

1 med.-sized eggplant	**1 egg**
Salt	**2/3 c. milk**
1 c. pancake mix	**2 tbsp. salad oil**

Peel the eggplant and cut in 1/2-inch slices. Cut the slices in half and cover with water and 1 tablespoon salt. Soak for several hours and drain well. Combine pancake mix, egg, milk and oil in a shallow bowl. Salt the eggplant slightly and dip in the pancake mix. Fry in deep fat for 2 to 3 minutes on each side. 6 servings.

Mrs. Lee Tschirhart, Castroville, Texas

CHOPPED EGGPLANT
20 minutes to prepare; 10 to 20 minutes to cook

1 eggplant	1 celery stalk
1 tomato	3 tbsp. butter
1 onion slice	1 c. water

Chop the eggplant, tomato, onion and celery. Heat the butter in a frypan and add the vegetables and water. Cook for 10 minutes or until vegetables are tender. 4 servings.

Mrs. F. B. Dunn, Donalsonville, Georgia

EGGPLANT PROVENCAL
Preparation and cooking time less than 1 hour

2 chopped eggplant	Pinch of dried tarragon
3 lge. tomatoes, chopped	2 green olives, chopped
Juice of 1 lemon	Salt and pepper to taste

Place the eggplant and tomatoes in a small saucepan and add the lemon juice, tarragon and olives. Simmer for 30 minutes, well covered, over low heat. Season and sprinkle with additional chopped olives, if desired. 2 servings.

Mrs. L. M. Knox, Port Arthur, Texas

STUFFED MUSHROOMS
20 minutes to prepare; 15 minutes to bake

12 lge. mushrooms	Dash of marjoram
2 tbsp. chopped celery	3 tbsp. fat
2 tbsp. chopped parsley	1/2 c. bread crumbs
1 tbsp. minced onion	1/2 c. cream
1/2 tsp. salt	

Place the mushroom caps upside down in a buttered baking dish. Chop the stems fine and blend with the celery, parsley, onion, salt and marjoram. Saute the celery mixture in fat until golden brown, then fold in the bread crumbs. Spoon into the mushroom caps and cover with the cream. Bake at 375 degrees for 10 to 15 minutes. 6 servings.

Janice M. Mountz, Rome, Georgia

Mushrooms with Rice (below)

MUSHROOMS WITH RICE
Preparation and cooking time about 30 minutes

1 10 1/2-oz. can beef consomme	1 tbsp. lemon juice
1 c. packaged precooked rice	1/4 c. butter
1/2 lb. fresh mushrooms, sliced	1/4 c. chopped onion
	1/4 c. chopped parsley

Combine the consomme and 1 3/4 cup water in a 1 1/2-quart saucepan and bring to a boil. Add the rice, cover and cook over low heat for about 25 minutes or until tender and all the liquid is absorbed. Toss the mushrooms with the lemon juice. Melt the butter in a small saucepan and add the mushrooms and onion and saute for 5 minutes. Toss the mushroom-onion mixture and the parsley with the rice just before serving.

MUSHROOMS POLONAISE
Elegant but quickly prepared; 20 minutes for cooking

4 tbsp. butter	Salt to taste
1 garlic clove, crushed	Freshly ground pepper to taste
1 lb. fresh mushrooms, sliced	1 c. sour cream
3 tbsp. finely chopped parsley	Buttered croutons

Place the butter in the top of a chafing dish over direct heat and add the garlic, mushrooms, parsley, salt and pepper. Cook until mushrooms are tender, then add the sour cream. Serve over hot buttered croutons.

Mrs. Wendall S. Palmer, Tidewater, Virginia

FRIED OKRA
20 minutes to prepare; 20 minutes to cook

3/4 tsp. salt	1/4 c. milk
1/4 tsp. pepper	1 c. bread crumbs
2 tbsp. flour	Bacon drippings
3 c. tender okra slices	Butter
2 eggs, well beaten	

Combine the salt, pepper and flour, then dredge the okra in the flour mixture thoroughly. Combine the eggs, milk, bread crumbs and okra. Melt a small amount of bacon drippings and butter in a frypan and add the okra mixture. Simmer for several minutes, then cover. Cook until brown, then turn to brown remaining side. 6-8 servings.

Mrs. F. W. Burks, Bedford, Virginia

CHEESY NUT ONIONS
Fancy yet easy to prepare; 20 minutes to cook

1/2 c. diced celery	1 tsp. dry mustard
2 tbsp. butter	1 1-lb. jar sm. whole onions
1/3 c. evaporated milk	3 tbsp. salted peanuts
1/4 lb. American cheese, grated	

Saute the celery in the butter until tender, but not brown, then add the milk, cheese and mustard. Continue cooking over low heat until well blended, stirring constantly. Drain the onions and add to the cheese sauce. Heat and garnish with the peanuts. 4 servings.

Mrs. Earl L. Faulkenberry, Lancaster, South Carolina

GOURMET ONIONS
Quickly prepared; 10 minutes cooking time

3 tbsp. butter	1/4 tsp. pepper
1/2 tsp. monosodium glutamate	1/4 c. sherry
1/2 tsp. sugar	1 can sm. onions, drained
Salt to taste	1/4 c. shredded Parmesan cheese

Melt the butter in a saucepan, then stir in the monosodium glutamate, sugar, salt, pepper and sherry. Add the onions and cook over high heat for about 5 minutes, stirring occasionally. Turn into a serving dish and sprinkle with Parmesan cheese. 4 servings.

Mrs. Earl M. Thompson, Waco, Texas

GINGER ONIONS
Emergency shelf ingredients; mix and cook for 15 minutes

1 No. 2 1/2 can white onions	1 tbsp. paprika
4 tbsp. honey	1/2 tsp. salt
2 tbsp. butter	1/4 tsp. ginger

Place the onions in a buttered shallow baking dish. Combine the honey, butter, paprika, salt and ginger in a saucepan and cook for 5 minutes, then pour over the onions. Bake at 325 degrees for 10 minutes or until well glazed. 8 servings.

Mrs. Velma Shaffer, Little Rock, Arkansas

FRENCH PEAS
Quickly prepared in less than 30 minutes

1 pkg. frozen green peas	4 sprigs of parsley
1/2 c. celery slices	2 slices bacon
1/2 c. small onions	2 tbsp. chopped pimento
1/2 tsp. salt	

Cook the peas, celery, onions, salt and parsley in a small amount of water until tender, then drain and remove the parsley. Fry the bacon until crisp, then crumble and set aside. Add a small amount of bacon fat and pimento to the peas mixture and pour into a serving dish. Garnish with the crumbled bacon. 6-8 servings.

Mrs. Bessie Kennedy, Baxley, Georgia

GREEN PEA POELON
Preparation and cooking time less than 30 minutes

2 pkg. frozen green peas	1 can cream of mushroom soup
1 lge. green pepper, chopped	2 c. grated Velveeta cheese
1 onion, chopped	1 sm. can pimento, diced
1 clove of garlic, chopped	1 c. diced mushrooms
1 stick butter	

Cook the green peas according to package directions and drain. Saute the pepper, onion and garlic in the butter until tender and add to the green peas. Heat and stir the soup in a saucepan until smooth and add the cheese, pimento and mushrooms. Pour over the green peas mixture and serve.

Mrs. Peggy Sisk Maddox, Hopkinsville, Kentucky

TINY ENGLISH PEAS AND MUSHROOMS IN BUTTER
Emergency shelf ingredients; mix and cook for 20 minutes

1 can tiny English peas	1 can sliced mushrooms
1 tsp. sugar	2 tbsp. butter
1/2 tsp. salt	

Partially drain the peas and pour into a saucepan. Add the sugar and salt and bring to a boil. Saute the mushrooms in the butter until brown. Pour the peas into a serving dish, then spoon the mushrooms over the peas.

Mrs. Ted Moore, Pocahontas, Tennessee

ACORN SQUASH WITH SLICED APPLES
Preparation and cooking time less than 1 hour

3 fresh acorn squash	Margarine
Salt to taste	Nutmeg to taste
2 or 3 fresh tart apples	

Cut the acorn squash in half and remove the seeds. Place, cut side down, in a baking pan with 1/2 cup boiling water and cover. Bake for 10 minutes and remove from oven. Peel, core and slice the apples. Place the squash, cut side up, in a baking dish and season with salt, then fill with the apple slices. Dot with margarine and sprinkle with nutmeg. Pour 1/2 cup boiling water in the dish. Bake for 30 minutes longer or until squash is tender.

Photograph for this recipe on page 98.

PLANTATION SQUASH
20 minutes to prepare; 20 minutes to bake

2 lb. squash
Salt and pepper to taste

1 can celery soup
1 can fried onion rings

Cook the squash in a small amount of boiling water with salt and pepper until tender, then drain and place in a casserole. Pour the celery soup over the squash and top with the onion rings, then cover with foil. Bake for about 20 minutes at 350 degrees.

Mrs. A. C. Flieg, Denison, Texas

SQUASH CROQUETTES
Partially prepared ahead and cooled; allow 20 minutes for cooking

3 c. canned squash, drained
2 egg yolks
6 tbsp. butter
1 tsp. salt

3/4 c. chopped pecans
1 c. fine bread crumbs
1 egg, slightly beaten
1 tbsp. milk

Mash the squash through a sieve. Beat the egg yolks until thick and combine with the squash, butter and salt in a saucepan. Cook and stir over medium heat for 5 minutes. Stir in the pecans, then cool. Shape the squash mixture into croquettes and roll in the bread crumbs. Dip into egg diluted with milk and roll again in crumbs. Fry in deep fat until golden brown and drain on paper towels. Serve hot.

Mrs. Richard Smith, Thomaston, Georgia

SWEET POTATOES WITH MERINGUE TOPPING
Preparation and cooking time about 45 minutes

2 lb. sweet potatoes
2 tbsp. butter or margarine
1/2 c. milk
1/4 tsp. nutmeg

Salt to taste
1/4 tsp. cinnamon
3 egg whites
6 tbsp. sugar

Cook the potatoes in boiling water until tender, then peel and mash. Add the butter, milk, nutmeg and salt and mix well. Turn into a buttered casserole and sprinkle with the cinnamon. Beat the egg whites until soft peaks form. Add the sugar and beat until stiff peaks form. Spoon over the sweet potato mixture. Bake at 400 degrees until the meringue is brown.

Photograph for this recipe on page 2.

Potato-Orange Cups (below)

POTATO-ORANGE CUPS
Preparation and cooking time about 1 hour

6 oranges	1/2 c. orange juice
2 c. cooked, mashed sweet potatoes	1 tsp. pumpkin pie spice
	1/4 c. chopped pecans
2/3 c. (firmly packed) brown sugar	1/2 c. raisins
1/4 c. butter, melted	6 marshmallows

Slice off the tops of the oranges and scoop out sections, then notch the rims. Mix remaining ingredients, except marshmallows, thoroughly and fill the orange cups. Bake in a 375-degree oven for 30 minutes. Top with marshmallows and bake until bubbly and browned.

SPICED FRIED SWEET POTATOES
Easily prepared and cooked in about 20 minutes

2 med. sweet potatoes	2 tbsp. sugar
Butter	1/4 tsp. ground cinnamon

Peel the sweet potatoes and cut in lengthwise slices about 1/4 inch thick. Fry in a generous amount of butter over medium heat until soft and brown. Mix the sugar and cinnamon and sprinkle over the potatoes. Serve at once.

Mrs. S. P. Baker, Comstock, Texas

BAKED TOMATOES
Elegant but quickly prepared; 20 minutes for baking

6 med. tomatoes	Worcestershire sauce
Salt to taste	Parmesan cheese

Cut the tomatoes in half and remove the core. Place in an oiled baking dish with cut side up and season with salt and several drops of Worcestershire sauce. Bake at 350 degrees until tender. Sprinkle generously with the cheese and bake for 3 to 4 minutes longer. 6 servings.

Maxine Gibson, Starke, Florida

FRESH VEGETABLE KABOBS
Easily prepared; cooking time less than 30 minutes

Fresh mushrooms	**Fresh sliced zucchini**
Fresh cherry tomatoes	**1 bottle Italian dressing**
Small onions, cut in half	

Marinate the mushrooms, tomatoes, onions, and zucchini in Italian dressing for several hours. Drain the vegetables and reserve marinade. Place the vegetables on skewers and place on a grill over low coals. Cook until vegetables are tender, turning and brushing with reserved marinade occasionally.

Photograph for this recipe on page 5.

TOMATO-OLIVE SAUTE
Prepared and cooked in about 20 minutes

1/4 c. butter or margarine	**1/2 c. sliced pimiento-stuffed**
1 clove of garlic, crushed	**olives**
2 pt. cherry tomatoes	**Dash of pepper**

Melt the butter in a large skillet and add the garlic. Cook for 30 seconds over medium heat. Add the tomatoes, olives and a dash of pepper. Cook, stirring occasionally, for 5 to 10 minutes or until the tomato skins begin to break. Serve with baked chicken. 6 servings.

Tomato-Olive Saute (above)

Sausage-Peanut Pilaf (page 130)

casseroles

Every homemaker knows that casseroles are marvelous time-savers — and in this section, you'll discover the most readily prepared recipes for casseroles, recipes shared with you by *Southern Living* homemakers. In the following pages are casseroles using meats . . . fish . . . shellfish . . . poultry . . . vegetables . . . even eggs and cereals.

For that particularly important meal, relax and plan to serve Tenderloin Tip Casserole. It's so elegant, so festive, no one will ever guess how easy it was to prepare! If seafood is a favorite in your home, why not please everyone and save yourself precious time by featuring Lobster and Mushroom Casserole . . . Deviled Crab Casserole . . . or any of these seafood recipes.

Are the ladies coming to lunch? Then delight them all with a Ham Puff Casserole or Chicken Clemenceau that is certain to please. Add a salad, rolls, and your favorite dessert, and you're ready for a much talked-about luncheon that takes a minimum of effort on your part.

These recipes are the pride and joy of the women who submitted them for publication. Every one has brought its originator warm compliments . . . requests for the recipe . . . and that feeling of satisfaction that comes to women who prepare foods their families and friends love. Why not enjoy that feeling yourself, now, when you prepare one of the timesaving casserole recipes awaiting you in the pages that follow?

Sesame Pastry-Topped Stew (below)

SESAME PASTRY-TOPPED STEW
Preparation and cooking time about 30 minutes

1 tbsp. minced onion	1 1-lb. 14-oz. can meatball
1/2 tsp. dry oregano leaves	stew
1/2 10-oz. package pie	1 egg white
crust mix	1 tbsp. sesame seed

Preheat oven to 400 degrees. Combine the onion, oregano and pie crust mix. Prepare the pastry according to. package directions and roll out the dough on a lightly floured board. Cut into eight 2-inch long ovals. Pour the meatball stew into a 6 x 10-inch baking dish. Bake for 10 minutes. Beat the egg white until frothy. Spread each pastry oval with egg white. Sprinkle sesame seed over top of pastry. Remove stew from oven and place the pastry ovals over the stew. Return to the oven and bake for 15 minutes longer. 3-4 servings.

TENDERLOIN TIP CASSEROLE
Preparation and cooking time less than 1 hour

3 lb. tenderloin tips, cut in	2 cloves of garlic, crushed
cubes	1 lb. mushrooms, sliced
2 1/2 tsp. salt	1/2 c. tomato puree
1/8 tsp. pepper	1 c. cream
Flour	1/4 tsp. hot sauce
2 tbsp. butter	1 tbsp. Worcestershire sauce
1 c. chopped onions	1 c. sour cream

Season tenderloin with 1/2 teaspoon salt and pepper and dredge with flour. Brown in butter in a skillet over high heat, then place in a 3-quart casserole. Cook onions in remaining butter in the skillet until tender. Add the garlic, 1 teaspoon salt and mushrooms and cook for 5 minutes or until mushrooms are tender. Add tomato puree and pour over tenderloin. Bake at 375 degrees for 30 minutes. Heat the cream, hot sauce, Worcestershire sauce and remaining salt in a saucepan until simmering, then stir in sour cream. Pour over tenderloin mixture and stir well. Bake for 5 minutes longer. 6-8 servings.

Mrs. Louis Morris, Weatherford, Oklahoma

CHEDDAR BEEF
Partially prepared ahead; allow 1 hour and 30 minutes for baking

1 lb. round steak, cut in cubes	1/2 c. grated Cheddar cheese
1/2 c. chopped onion	1 can cream of mushroom soup
1 c. diced celery	1/2 soup can water
4 or 5 lge. potatoes, sliced	Salt and pepper to taste

Cook the steak, onion and celery in small amount of fat in a skillet until brown. Place alternate layers of potatoes, steak mixture and cheese in 2-quart casserole. Mix the soup, water and seasonings and pour over casserole. Bake at 350 degrees for 1 hour and 30 minutes. 6 servings.

Mrs. Charles Glascow, Atlanta, Georgia

CARACAS
Emergency shelf ingredients; mix and cook for 30 minutes

1 pkg. dried beef	1 tbsp. Worcestershire sauce
1 tbsp. butter	1 c. grated cheese
1 No. 2 can tomatoes	3 eggs, slightly beaten
1 tbsp. chili powder	

Cook the dried beef in butter in a saucepan until frizzled and add the tomatoes, chili powder, Worcestershire sauce and cheese. Cook until most of the liquid has evaporated. Add the eggs and cook until eggs are set, stirring constantly. Serve on hot water corn cakes.

Mildred Mason, Cherokee, Alabama

SNOW CAPS
Quick leftovers dividend; 30 minutes cooking time

3/4 c. chopped onion	2 1/2 c. cooked green beans
1 tbsp. shortening	1 can tomato soup
1 1/2 lb. ground beef	2 c. mashed potatoes
1 tsp. salt	1 egg, beaten
1/8 tsp. pepper	

Saute the onion in shortening until golden. Add the ground beef, salt and pepper and cook until brown, then drain. Drain the green beans and combine with the ground beef mixture and the soup in a 1 1/2-quart casserole. Combine the mashed potatoes and the egg, mixing well. Drop mounds of mashed potatoes on top of the ground beef mixture. Bake at 350 degrees for 30 minutes. 6 servings.

Mrs. Paula Arnold, Charlotte, North Carolina

```
┌─────────────────────────────────────────────────────────┐
│                    QUICK PATIO DINNER                     │
│             Beef and Rice Casserole page 122              │
│        Coleslaw with Sour Cream Dressing page 35          │
│             Piccalilli Hot Bread page 177                 │
│               Mocha Mousse page 161                       │
└─────────────────────────────────────────────────────────┘
```

BEEF AND RICE CASSEROLE
Preparation and cooking time less than 1 hour

1 1/3 c. packaged precooked rice	1 lb. ground beef
3 tbsp. minced onion	1 tsp. salt
1 1/2 c. diced celery	Dash of pepper
2 tbsp. margarine	1 can tomato soup

Preheat oven to 375 degrees. Prepare the rice according to package directions. Saute the onion and celery in hot margarine until tender. Place the rice in a greased 1 1/2-quart casserole and top with the celery and onions. Combine the ground beef with salt and pepper and brown in remaining margarine in the skillet. Arrange on top of the celery. Combine the soup with 1/4 cup water and pour over the ground beef. Bake, uncovered, for 35 minutes. 6 servings.

Mary Sue Smith, Dubach, Louisiana

GROUND BEEF AND GREEN BEAN CASSEROLE
Partially prepared ahead; allow 30 minutes for baking

1 lb. ground beef	1 can tomato soup
1 sm. onion, diced	1 med. can cut green beans
1/2 tsp. salt	1 c. grated cheese

Cook the beef and onion in a skillet until brown. Add the salt, soup and beans and mix well. Place in a casserole and cover with cheese. Bake at 350 degrees for about 30 minutes. 5-6 servings.

Mrs. Burl Price, Erie, Tennessee

BEEF BAKE
Preparation and cooking time less than 1 hour

1 pkg. macaroni and cheese dinner	2 tbsp. margarine
1 lb. ground beef	1 can cream of mushroom soup
2 tbsp. chopped onion	1/2 c. milk

Prepare macaroni and cheese dinner according to package directions. Brown the ground beef and onion in margarine in a skillet and stir in soup and milk. Place half the macaroni and cheese dinner in a greased 1 1/2-quart casserole and add half the beef mixture. Repeat layers. Bake at 350 degrees for 25 minutes. 4-6 servings.

Mrs. Norma Faye Phillips, Deer Lodge, Tennessee

BAKED GRITS
Partially prepared ahead; allow 1 hour for baking

1 c. quick-cooking grits	1 c. grated cheese
1/4 c. butter or margarine	1/2 can mushroom soup
2 eggs, lightly beaten	Paprika
2 tbsp. milk	

Cook the grits according to package directions and add the butter. Mix the eggs and milk and stir into grits mixture. Stir in 1/2 cup cheese and soup and pour into a greased casserole. Sprinkle remaining cheese on top and sprinkle lightly with paprika. Bake in 350-degree oven until firm.

Mrs. Hugh Moreland, Starkville, Mississippi

VARIEGATED GRITS
Quick leftovers dividend; 30 minutes cooking time

6 slices bacon, diced	1 tsp. salt
1 c. diced onions	Dash of pepper
2 c. cooked grits	1 tomato, chopped

Fry the bacon in a skillet until crisp. Add the onions and cook until tender. Add the grits, salt and pepper and cook, stirring, for about 1 minute. Add tomato and pour into a casserole. Bake at 350 degrees until heated through. 6-8 servings.

Mrs. C. W. Lawrence, Robards, Kentucky

GARLIC RICE
Partially prepared ahead; allow 20 minutes for baking

1 c. rice	3/4 c. grated American cheese
1/2 tsp. garlic powder	1 c. mushroom soup
1 sm. onion, minced	1 c. cracker crumbs
1 4-oz. can mushrooms	Butter

Cook the rice according to package directions, adding garlic powder and onion to water. Add the mushrooms, cheese and soup and pour into a greased baking dish. Cover with cracker crumbs and dot with butter. Bake in 350-degree oven until brown.

Mary T. Hill, Petal, Mississippi

SHOPPING DAY CASSEROLE
Emergency shelf ingredients; mix and bake for 30 minutes

3 lge. cans spaghetti with meatballs	1 sm. can tomatoes
1 can mushrooms	Parmesan cheese

Combine the spaghetti with meatballs, mushrooms and tomatoes in a baking dish and sprinkle with Parmesan cheese. Bake at 350 degrees for 30 minutes.

Mrs. Jessie Gilliland, Muleshoe, Texas

BAKED MACARONI LUNCHEON
Preparation and cooking time less than 1 hour

1 c. cooked macaroni	1 tbsp. flour
1 No. 2 can green asparagus	3/4 c. milk
tips	1 c. grated American cheese
1 No. 303 can whole tomatoes	Salt and pepper to taste
4 tbsp. melted margarine	1/2 c. bread crumbs

Spread the macaroni in a buttered baking dish. Drain the asparagus, reserving juice. Arrange the asparagus on top of the macaroni. Drain the tomatoes and place over the asparagus. Place 2 tablespoons margarine in a saucepan and blend in the flour. Add the asparagus juice, milk and cheese, stirring constantly. Bring to a boil, then sprinkle with salt and pepper. Pour the sauce over the casserole and sprinkle top with crumbs. Pour remaining margarine over crumbs. Bake in a 350-degree oven until slightly brown and heated through. 6-8 servings.

Mrs. Lois B. Johnston, Leesville, Louisiana

GEORGIA'S MACARONI CASSEROLE
20 minutes to prepare; 25 minutes to bake

2 med. green peppers	1/2 pt. sour cream
2 med. onions	1 14-oz. can Italian tomatoes
1 tbsp. cooking oil	1/2 c. Parmesan cheese
1 8-oz. box elbow macaroni	Salt to taste

Slice the green peppers and onions and fry in oil for 5 minutes over medium heat. Cook the macaroni in boiling, salted water until done and drain. Combine the macaroni, fried vegetables, sour cream, tomatoes and cheese and season. Pour into a 4-quart casserole. Bake in 325-degree oven for 25 minutes. 4-6 servings.

Mrs. William R. Cameron, Orlando, Florida

NOODLES DE VENCI
Preparation and cooking time about 30 minutes

1 6-oz. package noodles	Salt to taste
1 16-oz. can stewed tomatoes	Parmesan cheese, grated
1 tbsp. catsup	

Cook the noodles according to package directions and drain. Combine the noodles, tomatoes, catsup and salt and pour into a baking dish. Bake at 300 degrees for about 15 minutes. Sprinkle with cheese just before serving. About 4 servings.

Cheryl Massey, Milford, Delaware

NOODLE PUDDING
Partially prepared ahead; allow 1 hour and 30 minutes to bake

1/2 lb. broad noodles	3 tbsp. sour cream
1/2 lb. cottage cheese	3 eggs, beaten

1/2 c. sugar	1 1/2 c. cold milk
Salt to taste	1 c. corn flake crumbs
1/8 lb. melted butter	1/2 tsp. cinnamon

Preheat oven to 350 degrees. Parboil the noodles and drain. Place a greased 8 x 11-inch pan in oven to heat. Combine the noodles, cottage cheese, sour cream, eggs, sugar, salt, butter and milk and pour into heated pan. Sprinkle with corn flake crumbs and cinnamon. Bake for about 1 hour and 30 minutes.

Mrs. Tom Jackson, Murfreesboro, Tennessee

PASTA HAM AND WALNUTS HAWAIIAN
Quick leftovers dividend; 45 minutes cooking time

1 1/2 c. cooked ham cubes	3 tbsp. all-purpose flour
2 c. cooked shell macaroni	1/2 tsp. salt
1 1/3 c. drained pineapple	1/2 tsp. ground ginger
tidbits	1 tsp. soy sauce
1/2 c. sliced red or green	1/4 tsp. pepper
seedless grapes	1 2/3 c. undiluted evaporated
1 c. toasted California	milk
walnut pieces	3/4 c. chopped California
3 tbsp. butter	walnuts

Combine the ham, macaroni, pineapple, grapes and walnut pieces. Melt the butter in a saucepan then stir in the flour, salt, ginger, soy sauce and pepper. Stir in the evaporated milk gradually and cook until thickened, stirring constantly. Add the sauce to the walnut mixture then pour into a 1 1/2-quart casserole. Bake at 350 degrees for about 20 minutes. Sprinkle the chopped walnuts around edge of casserole and return to oven for 10 minutes. 6 servings.

Pasta Ham and Walnuts Hawaiian (above)

TUNA SOUFFLE
Elegant but quickly prepared; 25 minutes for cooking

2 cans tuna	2 tbsp. melted butter
2 1/2 c. herb-seasoned stuffing mix	1 c. tomato juice
	3 eggs, separated

Combine the tuna, stuffing mix, butter, tomato juice and beaten egg yolks. Beat the egg whites until stiff and fold into the tuna mixture. Turn into a greased baking dish. Bake at 350 degrees for about 25 minutes. 4-6 servings.

Virginia T. Harbour, Arlington, Virginia

AFTER FIVE CASSEROLE
Partially prepared ahead; allow 20 minutes for cooking

2 tbsp. chopped onion	1 c. cooked cut green beans
1 tbsp. butter or margarine	1 tbsp. diced pimento
1 can cream of celery soup	1 7 3/4-oz. can salmon, drained
1/4 c. milk	
1/2 c. shredded mild process cheese	2 tbsp. buttered bread crumbs
2 c. cooked diced potatoes	

Cook the onion in butter until tender. Combine the soup and milk, stirring until smooth, then add to the onion. Add the cheese and cook and stir until melted. Add the potatoes, green beans and pimento. Pour 1/3 of the potato mixture into a 1-quart casserole. Break the salmon into chunks with 2 forks, then place half the salmon on top of the potato mixture. Repeat layers and top with remaining potato mixture. Sprinkle the crumbs on top. Bake at 400 degrees for 20 minutes. Garnish with chopped parsley, if desired. 4 servings.

After Five Casserole (above)

SALMON-CREAM CASSEROLE
20 minutes to prepare; 20 minutes to bake

8 oz. medium noodles	1 c. cream
1 pt. sour cream	1 1-lb. can salmon
1 pkg. onion soup mix	

Cook the noodles according to package directions and drain. Combine the sour cream with onion soup mix and blend well. Add the cream. Drain the salmon and break into chunks. Stir in the noodles and sour cream mixture and pour into a 2-quart casserole. Bake at 350 degrees for 20 minutes.

Mrs. Frank S. Wiggins, White Springs, Florida

DEVILED CRAB CASSEROLE
Prepare ahead and chill; allow 35 minutes for baking

1 lb. claw crab meat	1 tbsp. Worcestershire sauce
1 sm. box crackers, crumbled	1 tsp. prepared mustard
	1/2 bottle catsup
1/2 bell pepper, chopped	Dash of hot sauce
1/2 med. onion, chopped	Dash of pepper
3 hard-boiled eggs, grated	Dash of garlic salt
1 stick margarine, melted	1 tbsp. lemon juice
1 tbsp. mayonnaise	1 lge. can evaporated milk

Combine all ingredients in a casserole and refrigerate for 30 to 40 minutes. Bake at 400 degrees for 10 minutes. Reduce temperature to 350 degrees and bake for about 25 minutes longer.

Mrs. H. J. Jennings, Sylvester, Georgia

OYSTER AND STEAK CASSEROLE
Partially prepared ahead; allow 50 minutes for baking

1 lb. round steak, cut in cubes	Salt and pepper to taste
Flour	1 egg, beaten
1 pt. oysters	1 tbsp. catsup
Pastry for 2-crust pie	1 tbsp. lemon juice
1 1/2 c. sliced potatoes	1/8 tsp. mace

Dredge the steak with flour. Drain the oysters and reserve liquid. Line a 1 1/2-quart casserole with half the pastry and place alternate layers of steak, oysters and potatoes in pastry, seasoning each layer with salt and pepper. Add 1/4 cup reserved oyster liquid. Cover with remaining pastry, cutting hole in center, and brush with egg. Bake at 400 degrees for 10 minutes. Mix remaining reserved oyster liquid with catsup, lemon juice and mace and pour into casserole through hole in pastry. Reduce temperature to 350 degrees and bake for 40 minutes longer. 6 servings.

Shirley Cormney, Liberty, Kentucky

LOBSTER AND MUSHROOM CASSEROLE
Preparation and cooking time less than 30 minutes

1 lb. mushrooms	1/2 c. chicken bouillon
5 1/2 tbsp. butter	2 c. diced lobster
3 tbsp. flour	1/2 c. cream
1 tsp. salt	2 egg yolks
1/8 tsp. paprika	1/2 c. cooking sherry
1 1/2 c. milk	1/3 c. bread crumbs

Slice the mushrooms and saute in 4 tablespoons butter in a saucepan for 2 minutes. Add the flour, salt and paprika and cook and stir over low heat for 5 minutes. Stir in the milk and bouillon and cook and stir for 3 minutes. Add the lobster, cream, egg yolks and sherry and mix well. Pour into a greased casserole. Cover with bread crumbs and dot with remaining butter. Bake at 450 degrees for 10 minutes. 6 servings.

Mrs. William B. Jackson, Huntsville, Alabama

JIFFY SHRIMP DINNER
Quick leftovers dividend; 10 minutes cooking time

1 can frozen shrimp soup	1/2 tsp. salt
2/3 c. cooked rice	Dash of pepper
8 oz. cooked shrimp	1/2 c. diced green pepper
1/2 c. diced celery	1/4 c. toasted almonds

Place the soup in a skillet and add 3/4 cup boiling water, then stir in the rice. Add remaining ingredients except almonds and cover. Bring to a boil and cook for 10 minutes. Sprinkle with almonds just before serving. 4 servings.

Mrs. George Weeks, Columbus, Georgia

LAMB-PINTO STEW
Easily prepared; allow 1 hour for baking

2 lb. lamb shoulder, cut in cubes	1/2 tsp. thyme
1/4 c. flour	1 1/2 c. cooked pinto beans
3 tbsp. salad oil	1 12-oz. can whole kernel corn
1 med. onion, sliced	1 4-oz. jar pimento strips, drained
1 c. stock or bouillon	1 med. green pepper, cut in strips
1 tsp. salt	
1/2 tsp. pepper	
1/2 tsp. basil	

Coat the lamb with flour and brown in hot oil in a skillet. Remove lamb from skillet. Add onion to skillet and cook until golden. Stir in remaining ingredients and lamb and turn into lightly greased 2-quart casserole. Bake at 350 degrees for 1 hour or until lamb is tender, stirring occasionally. 8 servings.

Mrs. Edith Nance, Rockwood, Tennessee

LAMB AND BLACK-EYED PEAS
Preparation and cooking time about 1 hour

3 c. chopped cooked lamb	2 cloves of garlic, minced
2 cans black-eyed peas, drained	2 cans beef bouillon
1/2 lb. Polish sausage, chopped	Worcestershire sauce to taste
2 med. onions, chopped	2 pkg. frozen green beans

Saute the lamb in small amount of fat in a skillet until brown and place in a deep casserole. Add the peas. Brown the sausage, onions and garlic in the skillet and add to casserole. Add the bouillon and Worcestershire sauce and cover. Bake at 350 degrees for 40 minutes. Add the green beans and bake for 20 minutes longer. 8-10 servings.

Mrs. Eleanor Robbins, New Orleans, Louisiana

CANADIAN BACON CASSEROLE
Quickly prepared; allow 1 hour for baking

2 tbsp. flour	1/2 c. chopped onion
1/2 tsp. celery seed	1 roll garlic cheese, cut in
1/2 tsp. oregano	slices
Salt to taste	8 to 10 slices Canadian bacon
4 c. sliced potatoes	3/4 c. milk
1 No. 2 can French-style	1 tbsp. catsup
green beans	Dash of hot sauce

Mix the flour with celery seed, oregano and salt. Place the potatoes, beans, onion, cheese and bacon in layers in a casserole, sprinkling each layer with flour mixture. Combine the milk, catsup and hot sauce and pour over top. Cover. Bake at 350 degrees for 30 minutes. Remove cover and bake for 30 minutes longer. 6 servings.

Mrs. R. McConnell, Atlanta, Georgia

HAM PUFF CASSEROLE
Partially prepared ahead; allow 1 hour for baking

2 c. milk	1/4 tsp. salt
1 tbsp. butter	1/4 tsp. paprika
1/3 c. yellow cornmeal	1 c. grated cheese
3 eggs, separated	1 c. cooked ground ham

Place the milk and butter in a saucepan and bring to boiling point. Stir in cornmeal slowly and cook for 5 minutes, stirring constantly. Remove from heat and stir in the beaten egg yolks, salt and paprika. Add the cheese and stir until melted. Add the ham and fold in the stiffly beaten egg whites. Pour into a buttered 2-quart casserole. Bake at 325 degrees for about 1 hour or until a knife inserted in center comes out clean. 6-8 servings.

Mrs. Richard M. Anderson, Chatham, Virginia

GROUND PORK CASSEROLE
Quickly prepared; 1 hour baking time

2 eggs, slightly beaten	1 1/2 tsp. salt
3 c. ground cooked pork	1/4 tsp. pepper
1/2 c. rice	1/2 tsp. Worcestershire sauce
1 c. milk	

Combine all ingredients in a bowl and mix well. Turn into a casserole and cover. Bake at 350 degrees for 1 hour or until rice is tender. 5 servings.

Mary J. Davis, White Plains, Kentucky

CHOPS GERMAINE
Easily prepared; allow 1 hour for baking

5 med. potatoes, halved	Prepared mustard
Milk	Salt and pepper to taste
5 pork chops, 1 in. thick	Bread crumbs

Place the potatoes, cut side down, in a deep casserole and add enough milk to cover. Spread chops with mustard and sprinkle with salt and pepper. Place chops over potatoes and cover with crumbs. Cover. Bake at 350 degrees for 1 hour or until tender. 5 servings.

Mrs. C. B. Lawrence, El Paso, Texas

PORK CHOPS AND RICE
Easily prepared in 15 minutes; allow 1 hour for baking

4 lean loin pork chops	1 c. beef bouillon
1/4 c. rice	1/4 tsp. thyme
4 thick slices Bermuda onion	1/2 tsp. marjoram
4 thick slices fresh tomato	Salt and pepper to taste
4 thick rings green pepper	

Brown the pork chops in a skillet and place in shallow greased casserole. Place 1 tablespoon rice, 1 onion slice, 1 slice tomato and 1 green pepper ring on each chop and pour bouillon over all. Sprinkle with seasonings and cover. Bake at 350 degrees for about 1 hour.

Mrs. Ruth Morris, Durham, North Carolina

SAUSAGE-PEANUT PILAF
Partially prepared ahead; allow 30 minutes for baking

1 lb. fresh pork sausage	1/4 c. chopped green pepper
1 c. finely sliced celery	1/3 c. chopped salted
1/2 c. chopped onion	peanuts
1 c. cooked rice, drained	6 to 8 stuffed green olives,
1 can mushroom soup	sliced

Cook the sausage in a skillet until lightly browned. Add the celery and onion and cook for 3 minutes, then pour off the drippings. Add the cooked rice, soup and green pepper to the sausage mixture, then pour into a 1-quart casserole and sprinkle with the chopped peanuts. Bake at 350 degrees for 30 minutes. Serve topped with sliced olives. 4-6 servings.

Photograph for this recipe on page 118.

CHICKEN-CHEESE CASSEROLE
Quick leftovers dividend; 40 minutes baking time

1 c. diced celery	1/2 tsp. pepper
2 tbsp. diced onion	2 eggs, well beaten
2 tbsp. butter	3/4 c. hot milk or chicken
2 c. diced cooked chicken	stock
2 c. dry bread crumbs	1 c. grated Cheddar cheese
1 tsp. salt	

Saute the celery and onion in butter in a saucepan until tender. Add remaining ingredients except cheese and mix well. Place in a well-greased 8-inch square casserole and top with cheese. Bake at 325 degrees for 40 minutes. 8 servings.

Mrs. Omar Robinson, Meridian, Texas

DEVILED CHICKEN
Partially prepared ahead; allow 1 hour for baking

1 diced cooked chicken	2 cans cream of mushroom soup
6 hard-cooked eggs, diced	2 c. white sauce or chicken
2 c. chopped green peppers	broth
2 c. chopped celery	Salt and pepper to taste
2 lge. onions, chopped	Bread crumbs

Combine all ingredients except the bread crumbs and pour into a shallow baking pan. Cover with crumbs. Bake at 350 degrees for about 1 hour or until done.

Mrs. W. M. Gee, Whiteville, Tennessee

EASY CHICKEN WITH ONIONS
Elegant, but quickly prepared; 1 hour and 30 minutes to bake

1 lge. fryer, disjointed	1 can mushroom soup
1/2 tsp. salt	2 tbsp. cooking sherry
1/2 tsp. pepper	1/2 c. shredded sharp cheese
12 to 16 tiny onions	

Place the chicken in a shallow baking dish. Sprinkle with salt and pepper and add onions. Mix the soup and sherry and pour over chicken. Sprinkle with cheese and cover. Bake at 350 degrees for 45 minutes. Uncover and bake for 45 minutes longer.

Mrs. H. A. Maison, Winter Park, Florida

CHICKEN CLEMENCEAU
Preparation and cooking time less than 1 hour

1 chicken, disjointed	8 garlic slivers
Seasoned flour	1 4-oz. jar pimento, chopped
1 to 2 c. cooking oil	1 3 1/2-oz. can mushrooms
4 lge. potatoes, diced	1 to 2 tsp. salt
1 stick butter or margarine,	1 to 2 tsp. pepper
melted	1 4-oz. can peas

Dredge the chicken with seasoned flour. Brown in cooking oil in a skillet, then place in a casserole. Brown the potatoes in oil remaining in skillet and drain. Place in a baking pan. Combine butter and garlic and pour over potatoes. Add the pimento, mushrooms, salt and pepper and cover. Bake at 325 degrees for 30 minutes. Add the peas and toss lightly. Spoon over chicken and bake for 15 minutes longer. 4 servings.

Mrs. S. L. Russell, Jr., Metairie, Louisiana

CHICKEN AND SWEET POTATO
Quickly prepared; 1 hour baking time

1 fryer, disjointed	1/2 c. pineapple juice
Salt to taste	Brown sugar
2 med. sweet potatoes	Butter
6 to 8 slices canned pineapple	Cinnamon

Season the chicken with salt and place in a long, shallow, foil-lined casserole. Cut the sweet potatoes in 1/4-inch slices and place over chicken. Place the pineapple over sweet potatoes. Pour pineapple juice over top. Place 1/2 teaspoon brown sugar in center of each pineapple slice and dot with butter. Sprinkle with cinnamon and seal foil. Bake at 400 degrees for about 1 hour or until chicken is tender. 6 servings.

Imogene Huffman, Hattiesburg, Mississippi

GLAZED FRANKFURTER CASSEROLE
Emergency shelf ingredients; mix and cook for 20 minutes

2 1-lb. cans pork and beans	2 tbsp. brown sugar
with tomato sauce	1 tsp. prepared mustard
6 frankfurters	1 tsp. Worcestershire sauce

Pour the beans into a shallow baking dish. Cut the frankfurters almost in half and arrange on beans, cut side up. Combine the sugar, mustard and Worcestershire sauce and spread over the frankfurters. Bake at 450 degrees for 20 minutes or until beans are hot and frankfurters are browned. 4 servings.

Mildred Wood, Gaffney, South Carolina

CHILI CASSEROLE
Emergency shelf ingredients; mix and cook for 25 minutes

1 6-oz. package corn chips	1 8-oz. can seasoned tomato
2 c. shredded sharp cheese	sauce
1 15-oz. can chili with beans	1 tbsp. instant minced onion
1 15-oz. can enchilada sauce	1 c. sour cream

Reserve 1 cup corn chips and 1/2 cup cheese. Combine remaining chips and cheese with the chili, sauces and onion and pour into a casserole. Bake at 375 degrees for 20 minutes. Remove from the oven and spread top with sour cream. Sprinkle with reserved cheese and place remaining corn chips in a ring around edge. Bake for 5 minutes longer. 6 servings.

Sue Williamson, Alexandria, Virginia

BAVARIAN KRAUT AND FRANKFURTERS
Preparation and cooking time less than 30 minutes

4 c. undrained sauerkraut	2 c. prepared biscuit mix
2 c. beer	3/4 c. milk
1 med. onion, chopped	1 tbsp. poppy seed
1 bay leaf	1/2 lb. frankfurters
1 tsp. salt	1/2 lb. bratwurst
12 peppercorns	1/2 lb. bauernwurst

Combine the sauerkraut, beer, 2 cups water, onion, bay leaf, salt and peppercorns in a large kettle or Dutch oven and bring to a boil. Combine the biscuit mix, milk and poppy seed with a fork. Prick the meats with a fork and add to the kettle. Spoon the dough by tablespoonfuls on top. Cook, uncovered over low heat for 10 minutes, then cover and cook for 10 minutes longer. Serve the meat and dumplings with the sauerkraut, draining the sauerkraut, if desired. 6 servings.

Bavarian Kraut and Frankfurters (above)

133

```
┌─────────────────────────────────────────────────────────────┐
│              PANTRY SHELF CORNED BEEF SUPPER                  │
│           Onion-Crested Hash Casserole page 134              │
│            Congealed Vegetable Salad page 36                 │
│                   Popovers page 180                          │
│             Quick Bavarian Dessert page 158                  │
└─────────────────────────────────────────────────────────────┘
```

ONION-CRESTED HASH CASSEROLE
Easily prepared; allow 30 minutes for baking

4 c. sliced onions	2 15 1/2-oz. cans corned beef
3 tbsp. vegetable oil	hash
1/2 tsp. curry powder	1/3 c. milk
1 tsp. Worcestershire sauce	1/2 c. fresh bread crumbs
1/2 tsp. salt	1/2 c. grated Cheddar cheese
1/8 tsp. pepper	

Preheat oven to 375 degrees. Saute the onions in oil until golden. Remove from heat and sprinkle in curry powder. Mix Worcestershire, salt, pepper and hash and turn into a 1-quart baking dish. Pour the milk over the hash mixture. Top with onions. Toss the crumbs and cheese together and sprinkle over onion layer. Bake for 30 minutes. 6 servings.

Melanie Lane, Spartanburg, South Carolina

VEAL WITH ARTICHOKES
Preparation and cooking time about 1 hour

2 lb. boneless veal steaks	1/4 c. chopped shallots or
1 tsp. salt	onion
1/2 tsp. pepper	2 15-oz. cans artichoke
2 tbsp. olive oil	hearts
1/2 c. cooking sherry	Chopped parsley to taste

Preheat oven to 325 degrees. Cut the steaks in 6 portions and season with salt and pepper. Saute in oil in a heavy skillet until brown. Add sherry and shallots and cover. Cook for 10 minutes or until almost tender, then remove steaks from sherry mixture. Place alternating layers of veal and artichoke hearts in 2-quart casserole and pour sherry mixture over all. Cover. Bake for 40 minutes or until veal is tender. Remove cover and sprinkle with parsley. Serve immediately.

Mrs. C. I. Balcer, Phoenix, Arizona

ASPARAGUS EN CASSEROLE
Elegant but quickly prepared; 45 minutes for cooking

1/2 lb. sliced Canadian bacon	3 tbsp. butter
1 1/2 lb. fresh asparagus	3 tbsp. flour

1/2 tsp. salt
Dash of pepper
1/8 tsp. paprika
1 c. milk

1/2 tsp. prepared mustard
1 3-oz. can broiled
   mushrooms
1/2 c. grated American cheese

Brown the bacon in a skillet and place in 4 individual shallow baking dishes. Cook the asparagus in salted water until just tender and drain well. Arrange over bacon. Melt the butter in a saucepan and stir in the flour, salt, pepper and paprika. Add the milk, mustard and mushrooms and bring to a boil, stirring constantly. Pour over asparagus and sprinkle cheese over top. Bake at 425 degrees until heated through and browned.

Mrs. John F. McCloskey, Sanford, Florida

CORN CASSEROLE
Quickly prepared; 30 minutes cooking time

2 10-oz. packages frozen
   whole kernel corn
2 slices bacon
1/4 c. butter
1/2 tsp. marjoram
1/2 tsp. salt

1/4 tsp. pepper
1/4 c. chopped onion
1/4 c. chopped green pepper
2 lge. tomatoes, cut in
   wedges

Preheat the oven to 350 degrees. Defrost the corn at room temperature. Fry the bacon in a skillet, then drain and set aside. Pour off the bacon drippings and melt the butter in the skillet. Add the marjoram, salt, pepper, onion and green pepper and saute until tender. Add the corn and cook, stirring occasionally, for 5 minutes or until the corn is tender. Garnish with the tomato wedges and bacon strips. Bake for 15 to 20 minutes or until heated through. 5-6 servings.

Corn Casserole (above)

Oven-Easy Vegetable Medley (below)

OVEN-EASY VEGETABLE MEDLEY
Easily prepared; allow 1 hour for baking

1/2 c. butter	1 10-oz. package frozen
2 tbsp. sliced green onions	corn
1 clove of garlic, split	2 tomatoes, sliced
3/4 tsp. salt	1/3 c. fine dry bread
1 10-oz. package frozen	crumbs
lima beans	

Preheat oven to 350 degrees. Melt the butter in a small saucepan. Saute the onion and garlic for about 5 minutes or until the onion is tender. Remove the garlic, then add the salt and set the butter mixture aside. Break the frozen vegetables apart, then place the lima beans in a shallow 1 1/2-quart casserole. Add a layer of tomato slices, then a layer of all the corn. Top with remaining tomato slices. Reserve 2 tablespoons of the butter mixture, then pour remaining butter mixture over the vegetables. Cover tightly with foil. Bake for 50 minutes. Toss the bread crumbs with the reserved butter and sprinkle over the vegetables. Return to the oven and bake, uncovered, for 10 to 12 minutes longer. 6 servings.

CAULIFLOWER AND HAM CASSEROLE
Quick leftovers dividend; 40 minutes cooking time

1 cauliflower	Dash of pepper
3 tbsp. butter or margarine	1/2 lb. process cheese,
3 tbsp. flour	sliced
1 1/2 c. milk	1 c. chopped cooked ham
1/4 tsp. salt	1 c. soft bread crumbs

Separate the cauliflower into flowerets and cook in boiling, salted water until almost tender. Drain. Melt the butter in a saucepan and stir in flour. Add the milk, salt and pepper and cook, stirring, until thickened. Add the cheese and cook, stirring, until cheese is melted. Place cauliflower in a casserole and add the ham. Cover with cheese sauce and sprinkle crumbs around edge of casserole.

Bake at 350 degrees for 20 to 30 minutes or until crumbs are lightly browned. 6 servings.

Mrs. Clois C. Woolf, Piggott, Arkansas

EASY TO FIX GREEN BEANS
Emergency shelf ingredients; mix and bake for 30 minutes

1   1-lb. can green beans,
   drained
1 can cream of celery soup

2 tbsp. diced pimento
1/2 c. crushed potato chips

Combine the beans, soup and pimento and pour into a greased baking pan. Sprinkle with potato chips. Bake, uncovered, at 375 degrees for 20 to 30 minutes or until heated through. 4-6 servings.

Lucille Cook, Hutchins, Texas

BAKED SQUASH
Preparation and cooking time less than 1 hour

3 med. squash
1 sm. onion, chopped
1/2 tsp. salt
Pepper to taste

6 crackers, finely crushed
1 egg, beaten
Grated cheese

Cook the squash and onion with seasonings in enough water to prevent scorching until tender. Mash thoroughly and drain. Add cracker crumbs and egg to squash mixture. Pour mixture into a greased 2-quart baking dish. Bake in 350-degree oven for 30 minutes. Sprinkle with cheese and bake until cheese has melted. 6 servings.

Mrs. Tish Cupit, Alexandria, Louisiana

SWEET POTATO CASSEROLE
Easily prepared; 25 minutes baking time

1/2 c. (firmly packed) brown
   sugar
1/2 c. sugar
3 eggs, beaten
1 1/2 sticks margarine, melted

1 lge. can sweet potatoes,
   mashed
1 c. corn flake crumbs
1 c. chopped pecans

Combine the sugars, eggs, 1 stick margarine and potatoes. Mix the crumbs, remaining margarine and pecans. Place the potato mixture in a greased casserole and top with the corn flake mixture. Bake in 400-degree oven for 20 to 25 minutes. Serve hot. 6 servings.

Mrs. Jean Satterfield, Scottsboro, Alabama

Cheese-Noodle Casserole (page 148)

egg &
cheese
dishes

Eggs and cheese are two of the best friends today's time-conscious, budget-aware homemakers have. Low in cost, high in nutrients, and readily prepared in many ways, eggs and cheese are ideal for quick and easy cookery.

Eggs are often thought of as a breakfast dish, and the sparkling recipe for Brunch Egg Dish you'll find in this section is one you'll want to serve again and again. But don't limit eggs to morning meals. At your next luncheon, feature Deviled Eggs Delmonico . . . Luncheon Eggs with Mushrooms . . . or an Italian Omelet. Calorie-conscious diners will thank you — and everyone will love the marvelous flavor blends these dishes offer. You'll love them, too, because every elegant dish takes only minutes to prepare!

Serve cheese often. This protein-rich food cooks quickly and adds a delightful flavor and texture to every dish. Chateau Rainbow is a recipe you'll find in these pages — and once you serve it, you'll know why it was so popular with the family of the homemaker who shared it. An eye-appealing, palate-pleasing blend of cheese, peppers, noodles, peas, and carrots, this dish is just right for that in-a-hurry supper or rainy day lunch.

These are home-tested recipes, recipes especially created to please family members. Husbands appreciate the blending of flavors and hearty qualities of these dishes — and children enjoy them so much they're certain to ask for seconds. What greater compliment could you receive!

BAKED EGGS
Preparation and cooking time less than 1 hour

1/4 c. butter or margarine	2 c. milk
1/4 c. flour	1/2 lb. grated sharp cheese
1/2 tsp. salt	6 eggs

Melt the butter in a saucepan; then stir in the flour and salt until blended. Add the milk gradually, stirring until smooth. Add the cheese and stir until melted. Pour into a 1 1/2-quart casserole. Break the eggs into the sauce. Bake at 350 degrees until eggs are firm. 6 servings.

Mrs. Hilda Andersen, Grants, New Mexico

BRUNCH EGG DISH
20 minutes to prepare; 20 minutes to bake

1/4 c. butter	Garlic salt to taste
1/4 c. flour	1/4 tsp. thyme
1 c. half and half	1/4 tsp. marjoram
18 hard-boiled eggs, sliced	1 1/4 tsp. basil
1/2 lb. bacon, fried and	1/4 tsp. parsley
crumbled	Buttered crumbs
1 lb. Cheddar cheese, grated	

Melt the butter in a saucepan and blend in the flour. Stir in the half and half gradually. Cook and stir until thickened. Place the eggs, bacon, cheese and seasonings in a 3-quart casserole and mix lightly. Pour the sauce over the egg mixture and top with the crumbs. Bake at 350 degrees for 20 minutes. 10-12 servings.

Mrs. Ralph Wheeler, Greenbelt, Maryland

CINEMA EGGS
Preparation and cooking time less than 30 minutes

1 sm. can mushroom stems and	1 sm. onion, chopped
pieces	4 eggs, beaten

Drain the mushroom liquid into a skillet. Simmer the onion in the mushroom liquid until the liquid evaporates. Stir in the mushrooms and eggs and cook to desired doneness. 2 servings.

Mrs. Naomi Burrows, Fort Lauderdale, Florida

DEVILED EGGS DELMONICO
2 0 minutes to prepare; 25 minutes to bake

2 tbsp. grated onion	2 c. cooked macaroni
1/2 c. grated sharp cheese	10 deviled egg halves
1 1/2 c. thin white sauce	

Blend the onion, cheese, white sauce and macaroni and place in a greased 1-quart casserole. Press the deviled eggs into the macaroni mixture and cover casserole.

Bake in a 400-degree oven for about 25 minutes. Garnish with parsley, if desired. 4-6 servings.

Irene Malcolm, Neola, West Virginia

EGGS ADRIENNE
May be prepared ahead; allow 20 minutes to bake

3 c. buttered bread crumbs	2 cans cream of chicken soup
12 hard-boiled eggs, sliced	1/2 c. diced ham
Salt and pepper to taste	

Spread a portion of the bread crumbs in a baking dish and add a layer of egg slices. Season with salt and pepper and cover with soup. Add the ham and repeat layers of crumbs, eggs and soup, then top with crumbs. Bake in 350-degree oven until bubbly and browned. 12 servings.

Mrs. Tracy Wycoff, Danville, Virginia

EGGS BEAUREGARD
Preparation and cooking time less than 1 hour

1/2 c. butter	1/8 tsp. pepper
6 tbsp. flour	1/4 tsp. hot sauce
1 qt. milk	12 hard-cooked eggs, chopped
1 1/2 tsp. salt	1 c. grated cheese
1/2 tsp. paprika	8 rounds Holland rusk

Melt the butter over low heat, then add flour, stirring until bubbly. Add the milk and cook, stirring constantly, until smooth and thickened. Add remaining ingredients except cheese and Holland rusk and heat through. Add cheese just before serving. Serve on rounds of rusk. 8 servings.

Quinida Weeks, Aiken, South Carolina

EGGS IN TOMATO SAUCE
Partially prepared ahead; allow 45 minutes for baking

12 hard-boiled eggs, cut lengthwise	2 cans tomato soup
	4 lge. cans deviled ham
1/2 tsp. salt	2 sm. cans sliced mushrooms
1/4 c. chopped stuffed olives	1 1/2 c. grated sharp cheese
1/4 c. mayonnaise	1 tsp. seasoned salt

Remove the yolks from the eggs and mash, then add salt, olives and mayonnaise. Stuff the whites with yolk mixture. Place egg halves in single layer in a casserole and cover. Store in the refrigerator. Mix the soup, deviled ham, mushrooms, cheese and seasoned salt and pour over the eggs. Bake for 45 minutes at 350 degrees. 12-16 servings.

Odessa North, Portsmouth, Virginia

EGGS WITH CELERY SAUCE
Preparation and cooking time about 1 hour

7 tbsp. butter	1/2 c. chopped celery
6 tbsp. flour	1/4 c. chopped pimento
1 tsp. salt	12 hard-cooked eggs, quartered
3 c. milk	lengthwise
2 oz. blue cheese, crumbled	1/3 c. saltine cracker crumbs

Melt 6 tablespoons butter in a saucepan and blend in flour and salt. Add the milk and cook, stirring till thick. Stir in the cheese, celery and pimento. Place the eggs in a 12 x 7-inch baking dish and top with cheese sauce. Mix the cracker crumbs with remaining melted butter and sprinkle around edge of casserole. Bake in 325-degree oven for 45 minutes. 8 servings.

Mrs. David Purcell, Galveston, Texas

EGGS NEWPORT
Preparation and cooking time less than 1 hour

8 slices bacon	2 tsp. vermouth
1 can cream of mushroom soup	1 tsp. chopped chives
1/2 c. mayonnaise	6 hard-cooked eggs, sliced
1/2 c. milk	

Fry the bacon until crisp and drain on paper towels, then crumble. Blend the soup with mayonnaise and add the milk gradually, stirring until blended. Add the vermouth and chives and mix well. Layer the egg slices and mayonnaise sauce in a 1-quart baking dish, then sprinkle bacon around edge of dish. Bake at 350 degrees for 20 minutes. 4 servings.

Mrs. Emory Fairbanks, Pensacola, Florida

EGGS WITH CHEESE
20 minutes to prepare; 20 minutes to bake

3 tbsp. butter	2 c. milk
1/4 c. flour	3/4 c. grated Cheddar cheese
1 tbsp. salt	6 hard-cooked eggs, sliced
1/4 c. grated onion	1 c. buttered bread crumbs

Melt the butter in a saucepan, then blend in flour and salt. Add the onion and stir in the milk gradually. Cook and stir until thickened. Stir in the cheese. Arrange the egg slices in a casserole and pour in the cheese sauce. Top with the crumbs. Bake for about 20 minutes at 325 degrees. 4-5 servings.

Mrs. W. M. York, Murray, Kentucky

LUNCHEON EGGS WITH MUSHROOMS
20 minutes to prepare; 20 minutes to bake

6 hard-boiled eggs	4 tbsp. flour
1 c. chopped fresh mushrooms	2 c. milk
Butter	1 tsp. Worcestershire sauce
Salt and pepper to taste	1/4 c. shredded Cheddar cheese

Cut the eggs in half lengthwise. Remove and mash the yolks with a fork. Saute the mushrooms in 1/4 cup butter, salt and pepper until lightly browned and mix with mashed yolks. Fill the egg whites with the mushroom mixture and place in a greased shallow baking dish. Melt 4 tablespoons butter in a saucepan, then blend in the flour. Stir in the milk gradually. Add 1/2 teaspoon salt, Worcestershire sauce and cheese. Boil for 2 minutes over medium heat, stirring constantly and pour over eggs. Bake for 20 minutes at 325 degrees.

Mrs. J. B. Cameron, West Palm Beach, Florida

EASY HOLIDAY BRUNCH

Italian Omelet *page 143*
Fried Ham Slices *page 58*
Rosemary Biscuits *page 175*
Gardella Special *page 163*

ITALIAN OMELET
Elegant but quickly prepared; 20 minutes for cooking

1 8-oz. can tomato sauce with mushrooms	6 lge. eggs
1 tsp. Italian spice mix	Salt and pepper to taste
1/2 tsp. oregano	4-oz. mozzarella cheese, grated
1/2 tsp. sweet basil	4 tbsp. butter

Combine tomato sauce, spice mix, oregano and basil in a saucepan and simmer for 15 minutes. Beat the eggs lightly with salt and pepper, then add the cheese. Melt the butter in a frypan on low heat. Pour egg mixture in frypan and cook until edges brown. Fold omelet over and cook until set. Pour the tomato sauce over individual omelet servings. 4 servings.

Mrs. Harold Wilpan, Altus, Oklahoma

SPANISH EGGS
Preparation and cooking time less than 1 hour

1 6-oz. package noodles	1/4 lb. grated cheese
1/2 c. chopped onion	1/4 c. butter
1/2 c. chopped green pepper	1/4 c. flour
3 tbsp. fat	1/2 tsp. salt
2 1/2 c. tomatoes	6 hard-cooked eggs

Cook the noodles according to package directions, then drain and set aside. Cook the onion and green pepper in fat until tender. Add the tomatoes and simmer for 10 minutes. Add the cheese. Melt the butter in a saucepan and blend in flour and salt. Stir in the tomato mixture and cook, stirring until thickened. Place half the noodles in a baking dish. Slice 3 eggs over the noodles. Pour in half the tomato mixture. Repeat layers. Bake at 350 degrees for 25 minutes. 6-8 servings.

Mrs. S. L. Stacy, Greensboro, North Carolina

BACON-FILLED OMELET
Elegant but quickly prepared; 20 minutes for cooking

8 slices bacon	1/4 c. chopped green onions
4 eggs, beaten	2 tbsp. margarine
1/4 c. milk	Grated cheese
1/4 tsp. salt	

Preheat the oven to 350 degrees. Fry the bacon in a skillet until crisp, then drain and crumble. Combine the eggs, milk, salt and onions in a bowl. Melt the margarine in the skillet and sprinkle in the cheese to cover the bottom. Cook for 30 seconds to allow the cheese to partially melt, then pour in the egg mixture. Cook until the egg mixture is set, then place in the oven. Bake for 5 minutes or until the top is dry. Sprinkle the bacon over omelet, then cut across the center lightly with a table knife and fold the omelet. Slip onto a serving platter and garnish with spinach leaves and cherry tomatoes.

SWISS EGGS
Quickly prepared; 30 minutes baking time

1 c. grated American cheese	Dash of pepper
2 tbsp. butter	1 tbsp. prepared mustard
1/2 c. cream	6 eggs, slightly beaten
1/4 tsp. salt	

Spread the cheese in a well-buttered shallow baking dish and dot with butter. Combine the cream, salt, pepper and mustard. Pour half the cream mixture over the cheese. Pour the eggs into the baking dish and cover with remaining cream mixture. Bake in 350-degree oven for 25 to 30 minutes. 6 servings.

Sylvia Elgin, Tucson, Arizona

BAKED SPINACH-RICE AND CHEESE
Quick leftovers dividend; 25 minutes baking time

1 10-oz. package frozen spinach	2 tbsp. butter, melted
1 c. cooked rice	1/3 c. milk
1 c. shredded sharp cheese	2 tbsp. chopped onion
2 slightly beaten eggs	1/2 tsp. Worcestershire sauce
	1 tsp. salt

Cook the spinach according to package directions and drain. Blend all the ingredients together and pour into a greased 1-quart casserole. Bake at 350 degrees for 25 minutes or until inserted knife comes out clean. 6 servings.

Mrs. Lewis Koerselman, Sr., Spearman, Texas

CHEESE PIE
Easily prepared; allow 30 minutes for baking

3 eggs, well beaten	1 c. grated sharp cheese
1/2 tsp. salt	1 9-in. unbaked pie shell
1/2 c. evaporated milk	

Bacon-Filled Omelet (page 144)

Combine the eggs, salt, milk and cheese and pour into the pie shell. Bake at 325 to 350 degrees for about 30 minutes or until crust is done. Serve hot. 6 servings.

Sidelle D. Ott, Columbia, South Carolina

CHATEAU RAINBOW
Emergency shelf ingredients; mix and bake for 30 minutes

2 tbsp. diced red and green
  pepper
3 tbsp. butter
4 tbsp. flour
Mustard to taste
3 c. milk
8 oz. grated American cheese

8 oz. medium noodles, cooked
1 No. 2 can peas, drained
1 No. 2 can shoestring carrots,
  drained
3/4 tsp. salt
Dash of white pepper

Saute the pepper lightly in the butter, then blend in the flour. Add the mustard and stir in the milk gradually. Cook and stir until thick. Reserve a small amount of cheese topping and add remaining cheese to the sauce. Place the noodles, peas, carrots and seasonings in a buttered casserole and add the cheese sauce. Toss to mix, then top with reserved cheese. Bake at 350 degrees for 30 minutes. 6 servings.

Mrs. T. W. Taylor, Glenwood, Arkansas

CHEESE SOUFFLE
Prepare ahead; allow about 1 hour for baking

10 slices day-old bread	2 1/2 c. milk
3/4 lb. New York State cheese, grated	1 tbsp. grated onion
	1 tsp. salt
4 beaten eggs	1/2 tsp. dry mustard
1/2 tsp. Worcestershire sauce	Dash of cayenne pepper

Trim the crust from the bread, then place alternate layers of bread and cheese in a baking dish. Mix remaining ingredients and pour over bread and cheese. Bake at 325 degrees for 40 minutes or until set. May be prepared ahead and kept in refrigerator until time for baking. 8 servings.

Mrs. Alex A. Marks, Montgomery, Alabama

CHEESE TIMBALES
Quickly prepared; baking time less than 1 hour

4 eggs, lightly beaten	10 drops of onion juice
1 c. milk	1/2 c. grated American cheese
1/2 tsp. salt	
1/8 tsp. pepper	

Preheat oven to 350 degrees. Combine all the ingredients and stir until well mixed. Pour into buttered molds and set in a pan of hot water. Bake until firm. Remove to hot platter and serve with cream or tomato sauce. 6 servings.

Ramona Winters, Pine Bluff, Arkansas

EASY-DO MACARONI AND CHEESE
Partially prepared ahead; allow 30 minutes for cooking

1 8-oz. package elbow macaroni	4 hard-cooked eggs, diced
2 cans cream of chicken soup	2 tbsp. butter
1 can mushroom soup	1/2 lb. Edam cheese, diced
1/3 c. chopped onion	Paprika
2 tbsp. chopped pimento	

Prepare the macaroni according to package directions. Combine the macaroni, soups, onion, pimento, eggs, butter and cheese, reserving 1/2 cup cheese. Toss together lightly. Place in a 2-quart casserole and top with reserved cheese and paprika. Bake in 350-degree oven for 30 minutes. 10-12 servings.

Mrs. J. Gerald Sams, Arden, North Carolina

MANICOTTI-CHEESE BAKE
Preparation and cooking time less than 1 hour

1/2 lb. ground beef	2/3 c. tomato paste
1/2 c. minced onion	2 c. water
1/4 c. chopped green pepper	1 1/2 tsp. salt

1/2 tsp. pepper	1 pkg. small manicotti shells
1 tsp. sugar	2 c. ricotta cheese
1 1/2 tsp. Italian seasoning	1 c. shredded mozzarella cheese

Saute the ground beef, onion and green pepper for 10 minutes and drain fat. Add tomato paste, water, salt, pepper, sugar and seasoning and simmer for 15 minutes. Parboil manicotti in 4 cups salted water for 4 minutes, then drain on paper towels. Combine the cheeses and fill the manicotti shells. Place the filled shells in a greased shallow baking dish and cover with the ground beef sauce. Bake at 350 degrees for 20 to 30 minutes. 4 servings.

Mrs. L. M. Temple, Dillon, South Carolina

SWISS CHEESE SOUFFLE
Elegant but easily prepared; 1 hour and 20 minutes for cooking

1/3 c. butter	1 1/2 c. milk
1/4 c. flour	2 tsp. Worcestershire sauce
1 1/2 tsp. salt	2 c. finely shredded Swiss
1/2 tsp. paprika	cheese
1/8 tsp. pepper	6 eggs, separated

Melt the butter in a saucepan over low heat and blend in the flour, salt, paprika and pepper. Add the milk, stirring constantly, and cook until the sauce is smooth and thickened. Remove from heat and add the Worcestershire sauce and cheese gradually, stirring just until the cheese is melted. Cool slightly. Beat the egg yolks until thick and lemon colored and fold into the cheese mixture. Beat the egg whites until soft peaks form and fold into the cheese mixture. Pour into an ungreased 2-quart souffle dish or casserole. Set in a shallow pan of hot water. Bake at 350 degrees for about 1 hour or until silver knife inserted in center comes out clean. 8 servings.

Swiss Cheese Souffle (above)

CHEESE-NOODLE CASSEROLE
Partially prepared ahead; allow 25 minutes for baking

1/4 c. butter	1 8-oz. package pasteurized
3 tbsp. flour	process Swiss cheese,
3/4 tsp. salt	shredded
1/4 tsp. garlic salt	3 c. cooked noodles
1/8 tsp. white pepper	2 tbsp. sliced green onion
Dash of nutmeg	2 tbsp. diced pimento
2 c. milk	1/2 c. shredded Parmesan
1/2 c. dry white cooking	cheese
wine	

Melt the butter in a saucepan and blend in the flour, salt, garlic salt, pepper and nutmeg. Add the milk and cook, stirring constantly, until the sauce is smooth and thickened. Add the wine and Swiss cheese and stir until the cheese is melted. Fold the cooked noodles, green onion, pimento and 1/4 cup Parmesan cheese into the sauce. Pour the noodle mixture into a 1 1/2-quart shallow casserole. Sprinkle with remaining Parmesan cheese. Bake at 350 degrees for 25 minutes or until bubbly around the edges. 6 servings.

Photograph for this recipe on page 138.

GREEN CHILIES WITH CHEESE
Quickly prepared; 1 hour baking time

1 qt. cottage cheese	3/4 lb. Jack cheese, sliced
1 3-oz. can green chilies	3 or 4 eggs, well beaten

Spread the cottage cheese in a 2-quart casserole. Wash and drain the chilies, then cut and remove the seeds. Spread over the cottage cheese. Place cheese slices over the chilies and pour eggs over all. Bake at 350 degrees for 1 hour. 4 servings.

Mrs. John Thompson, Memphis, Tennessee

GOLDEN CHEESE AND RICE
Quick leftovers dividend; 40 minutes baking time

2 c. cooked rice	1 1/2 tsp. salt
3 c. shredded carrots	2 tbsp. onion flakes
2 c. grated cheese	1/2 c. milk
2 eggs, beaten	

Combine all the ingredients and toss to mix well. Place in a buttered casserole. Bake at 350 degrees for 35 to 40 minutes. 6 servings.

Mrs. B. C. Burdette, New Castle, Delaware

TOMATO-CHEESE DISH
Partially prepared ahead; allow 30 minutes to bake

8-oz. elbow macaroni	1 can tomato soup
2 tbsp. butter	1 sm. can tomato sauce

1 c. chopped Velveeta cheese	Salt and pepper to taste
1 c. chopped mozzarella cheese	4 slices American cheese

Cook the macaroni according to package directions, then drain and place in a greased casserole. Stir in the butter until melted. Mix in tomato soup and tomato sauce. Stir in the chopped cheeses, salt and pepper, mixing thoroughly. Lay the cheese slices on top. Bake at 350 degrees for 30 minutes. 4-6 servings.

Mrs. Harry Spencer, Las Vegas, New Mexico

CAMPERS' SPECIAL
Preparation and cooking time about 1 hour and 30 minutes

1 1-lb. 13-oz. can cling peach halves	4 c. elbow macaroni
1 tsp. salt	1/2 lb. grated Cheddar cheese
1/2 lb. bacon, cut in half	1 med. size onion, chopped
	1/4 tsp. garlic salt

Drain the peaches, reserving the syrup. Add water to the syrup to make 4 cups liquid. Add salt to the syrup mixture. Fry the bacon in a large skillet until partially done, then remove half the bacon. Add half the macaroni, half the cheese and the chopped onion, then add the reserved bacon and macaroni, all but 1/2 cup cheese. Pour the syrup mixture over all. Cover and cook over low heat for at least 1 hour. Remove the cover and stir in the reserved cheese. Add the peach halves. Bake for 10 to 15 minutes or until peaches are hot.

Campers' Special (above)

desserts & beverages

Southerners have a sweet tooth — every meal served southern-style invariably ends with a tasty dessert. To please their families, generations of southern women have turned their creative cooking artistry in the direction of desserts — and what marvelous recipes have resulted. Now those recipes that are easiest to prepare — without sacrificing the flavor that has made them famous — are shared with you in this section.

You'll find recipes so delicious your family will beg you to prepare them often. Chocolate Upside-down Cake is an old favorite with new taste, and Picnic Pound Cake is one of the South's most popular and well-known cakes. But cakes are just the beginning of what you'll find in these pages. There are refrigerator desserts like Cold Lemon Souffle . . . cakes such as Gold Rush Brownies . . . an elegant Tortoni with Strawberry Sauce .

Complementing the section on desserts is a delightful collection of great — and readily prepared — southern punches. Imagine how proud you'll be to feature Coffee Punch — or any one of the delicious recipes you'll discover in these pages.

Home-tested, family-approved, these are the dessert and beverage recipes which have brought fame and approval to the women who created them. Try one now — and discover for yourself how easy it is to please with these quick and easy desserts and beverages.

151

LEMON AND STRAWBERRY BOWL
Mixed in 5 minutes

1 bottle rose wine
2 lge. bottles ginger ale

1 lemon, sliced
1 pkg. frozen strawberries

Mix the wine and ginger ale in a punch bowl. Add the lemon slices and strawberries, stirring carefully until the strawberries are thawed. Add ice cubes, if needed.

Photograph for this recipe on page 150.

COFFEE PUNCH
Prepare ahead; chill until serving time

8 tbsp. instant coffee
2 c. sugar
3 qt. hot water
2 qt. milk

1 tbsp. vanilla
1 sm. can chocolate syrup
4 qt. vanilla ice cream

Mix the coffee, sugar and water and cool. Add the milk, vanilla and syrup and refrigerate overnight. Break the ice cream into chunks and add to the punch mixture 30 minutes before serving. 40 servings.

Mrs. R. H. Hammond, Jr., Miami Springs, Florida

ORANGE BLOSSOM COOLER PUNCH
Fancy, yet easy to prepare in 10 minutes

2 6-oz. cans frozen lemonade
1 6-oz. can frozen orange
   juice
9 c. cold water
5 pt. pineapple sherbet

1 qt. cherry vanilla ice cream
2 qt. ginger ale
Orange slices (opt.)
1 sm. jar sliced cherries (opt.)

Combine the frozen lemonade, orange juice and water. Place the sherbet and ice cream in a punch bowl and break into small pieces with a large spoon. Add the juice mixture and stir until sherbet and ice cream are partially melted. Add the ginger ale just before serving. Float orange slices centered with cherries to resemble blossoms. 50 servings.

Mrs. Milton L. Dominy, Nederland, Texas

RACY RED PUNCH
Partially prepared ahead; mix at serving time

1 46-oz. can pineapple-
   grapefruit drink
1/4 c. red cinnamon candies

1/3 c. sugar
1 qt. ginger ale, chilled

Heat 1 cup fruit drink and add cinnamon candies and sugar. Stir until dissolved, then add remaining fruit drink. Chill and add ginger ale just before serving. 2 1/2 quarts.

Mrs. Robert E. Finley, Charlotte, North Carolina

BERNA'S CHOCOLATE TART
Preparation and cooking time less than 1 hour

2 eggs, beaten	2 tbsp. cocoa
1/2 c. melted butter	2 tsp. baking powder
1 1/4 c. sugar	1/2 c. milk
1 1/4 c. flour	2 tsp. vanilla

Beat the eggs, butter and sugar together until foamy. Combine the flour, cocoa and baking powder and stir into the sugar mixture alternately with the milk. Add the vanilla. Grease a cake mold well and sprinkle with fine bread crumbs. Pour the batter into the prepared mold. Bake at 375 degrees for about 30 minutes or until cake tests done. Let cool.

Icing

1 c. confectioners' sugar	3 to 4 tbsp. strong coffee
1 tbsp. cocoa	4 tbsp. melted butter
2 tsp. vanilla	

Combine the sugar and cocoa and mix well, then add remaining ingredients. Stir until well mixed, then spread over the cake. Decorate with almonds or tinted sugar.

Berna's Chocolate Tart (above)

153

CHOCOLATE UPSIDE-DOWN CAKE
Easily prepared, allow 40 minutes for baking

3/4 c. dark corn syrup	2/3 c. chopped pecans
1/3 c. (firmly packed) dark	1 pkg. fudge cake mix
brown sugar	1 egg
1/4 c. margarine	3/4 c. water
1/8 tsp. salt	1/2 c. chocolate chips

Preheat oven to 350 degrees. Combine the corn syrup, sugar, margarine and salt in a saucepan and bring to a boil, stirring until margarine is melted. Remove from heat and stir in the pecans. Pour into a 9 x 9 x 2-inch baking pan and cool. Mix the cake mix, egg and water. Sprinkle the chocolate chips over the pecan mixture in pan, then pour in the batter. Bake for 35 to 40 minutes. Turn out onto serving plate immediately. Serve warm with whipped cream. 9 servings.

Mrs. John Hansbrough, Magee, Mississippi

DAFFODIL CAKE
Emergency shelf ingredients; mix and bake for about 50 minutes

4 eggs	1 c. milk
1 pkg. lemon cake mix	1 pkg. instant lemon pudding
1/2 c. corn oil	1 tbsp. grated lemon rind

Place all the ingredients in a large bowl and mix at medium speed for 2 minutes or 350 strokes by hand. Pour into a greased and floured 10-inch tube pan. Bake at 350 degrees for 45 to 50 minutes. Frost immediately with a glaze topping, if desired. 16 servings.

Mrs. Hazel Glencross, Jackson, Mississippi

PICNIC POUND CAKE
Easily prepared; allow about 1 hour to bake

2 sticks margarine or butter	1/2 tsp. baking powder
7 tbsp. vegetable shortening	1 c. milk
3 c. sugar	1/4 tsp. vanilla
5 eggs	1/4 tsp. almond extract
3 c. cake flour	

Cream the margarine, shortening and sugar in a bowl. Add the eggs, one at a time, beating well after each addition. Sift the flour and baking powder together and add to creamed mixture alternately with milk. Add the flavorings and mix well. Pour into a greased and floured tube pan. Bake at 350 degrees for about 1 hour or until cake tests done.

Mrs. Bob Glass, Pensacola, Florida

PUMPKIN CAKE
Quickly prepared; 45 minutes baking time

1 pkg. spice cake mix	3/4 c. finely chopped nuts
2 eggs	1/4 c. chopped dates
3/4 c. canned pumpkin	

Place the cake mix in a large mixing bowl and add the eggs. Add 1/4 cup less water than package directions require, then add the pumpkin and mix. Stir in the nuts and dates and pour into a greased tube pan. Bake at 350 degrees for 40 to 45 minutes. Drizzle with lemon sugar glaze, if desired. 12-14 servings.

Mrs. Evangelina L. Barber, Saluda, North Carolina

QUICK FUDGE CAKE
Preparation and cooking time less than 1 hour

1 pkg. chocolate pudding mix
1 pkg. devil's food cake mix
1/2 c. chopped walnut meats

1/2 c. semisweet chocolate pieces

Preheat oven to 350 degrees. Grease and flour a 13 x 9 1/2 x 2-inch pan. Prepare pudding mix according to package directions. Blend the dry cake mix into the hot pudding and pour into the prepared pan. Sprinkle with walnuts and chocolate bits. Bake for 30 to 45 minutes. Serve with whipped cream, if desired.

Mrs. Eva Russell, Dothan, Alabama

APRICOT GATEAU
Preparation and cooking time less than 1 hour

1 pkg. gingerbread mix
1 lge. can apricot halves

1 c. heavy cream
Chocolate decorettes

Prepare the gingerbread cake according to package directions and pour into a square pan. Bake according to package directions and cool. Cut in half to form 2 layers. Drain the apricots, reserving 1/4 cup liquid. Place half the apricots on 1 layer and top with the second layer. Whip the cream and reserved apricot liquid until stiff. Spread the whipped cream over the top and sides. Top with the remaining apricot halves and sprinkle with the chocolate.

Apricot Gateau (above)

COFFEE MALLO
Elegant but quickly prepared; chill until serving time

16 marshmallows
1/2 c. hot strong coffee

1 c. whipping cream, whipped

Melt the marshmallows in the coffee and let stand for 1 hour or until thickened. Fold in the whipped cream and pour in parfait glasses. Refrigerate until ready to serve. 6 servings.

Mrs. Stuart Henry Smith, Norfolk, Virginia

COLD LEMON SOUFFLE
Prepare ahead; chill until serving time

1 pkg. unflavored gelatin
3 eggs
Juice of 1 1/2 lemons

1/2 c. sugar
Pinch of salt
1/4 c. cream, whipped

Sprinkle the gelatin over 1/4 cup cold water in the top of a double boiler, then stir to dissolve over boiling water. Beat the eggs until creamy, then add the lemon juice, gelatin, sugar and salt. Fold in the whipped cream and turn into a serving dish and chill until ready to use. Serve with cream, if desired. 6 servings.

Mrs. Frank W. Norris, Norfolk, Virginia

ORANGE JELLY
May be prepared hours ahead and chilled until serving time

1 1/2 env. unflavored gelatin
2 1/2 c. orange juice

Juice of 1/2 lemon
Sugar to taste

Soften the gelatin in about 1/4 cup cold water, then dissolve in 1/2 cup hot water. Mix the gelatin with the juices and sugar and pour into serving dishes or dessert glasses. Chill until firm. Garnish with fruit and whipped cream, if desired. 4 servings.

ORANGE ICE CREAM WITH PRESERVED ORANGE PEELS
Ready to serve at any time

1 pt. orange ice cream

2 tbsp. preserved orange peels

Spoon the ice cream into individual dishes and garnish with the orange peels. 4 servings.

ORANGE SALAD
Prepare ahead; chill until serving time

1/2 c. water
1 tbsp. sugar

4 oranges

Combine the water and sugar and bring to a boil, then set aside to cool. Peel and thinly slice the oranges. Place the slices in a bowl and cover with the syrup. Garnish with orange slices. Serve cold. 4 servings.

ORANGE RICE
Preparation and cooking time about 30 minutes

1/2 c. rice	1 1/4 c. sweetened whipped
4 oranges	cream
Sugar	

Boil the rice in 2 cups water for about 20 minutes, then drain and rinse in cold water. Peel the oranges and cut 3 oranges in sections, then cut in pieces. Alternate the orange pieces with sugar in a bowl. Mix the rice, oranges and cream in a bowl. Slice the remaining orange and decorate the rice mixture. 4 servings.

ORANGE BLANCMANGE
Prepare ahead; chill until serving time

1 env. unflavored gelatin	1 1/4 c. whipped cream
4 oranges	1 tsp. vanilla
Sugar	

Soften the gelatin in 1/4 cup cold water. Peel and section the oranges, removing the seeds. Cut the orange sections in pieces and reserve a portion for garnish. Alternate the remaining orange pieces in serving dishes with layers of sugar. Whip the cream with 1/2 tablespoon sugar and the vanilla. Dissolve the gelatin in 1/2 cup hot water, then let cool. Mix the gelatin and the whipped cream well. Spread over the fruit mixture in the individual dishes and chill. Garnish with the reserved oranges. Cut horizontal slices of unpeeled orange and twist for a more decorative garnish. 4 servings.

Clockwise from top left: Orange Jelly (page 156), Orange Ice Cream with Preserved Orange Peels (page 156), Orange Rice (above), Orange Salad (page 156), Orange Blancmange (above)

STRAWBERRY WHIP
Prepare ahead; chill until serving time

1 env. unflavored gelatin	1 c. strawberry puree
1/4 c. sugar	2 tbsp. lemon juice
1/4 tsp. salt	1 tsp. grated lemon peel
2 egg whites	

Soften the gelatin in 1/4 cup cold water, then add the sugar, salt and 3/4 cup boiling water. Stir until dissolved. Chill the gelatin mixture until partially set. Beat the egg whites until stiff and fold into the gelatin mixture. Add the strawberry puree, lemon juice and peel and pour into a 1 1/2-quart mold or 6 individual molds. Top with whipped cream, if desired.

Mrs. Edmund Miller, Portales, New Mexico

QUICKIE BAVARIAN DESSERT
May be prepared hours ahead; chill until serving time

1 env. unflavored gelatin	1 tbsp. lemon juice
1/4 c. sugar	1 pkg. dessert topping mix
1 6-oz. can frozen grape juice	

Soften the gelatin in 1 cup cold water, then dissolve over low heat, stirring constantly. Remove from heat, and stir in the sugar, grape juice and lemon juice. Chill until partially congealed. Prepare dessert topping according to package directions. Beat the gelatin mixture until foamy, then fold in topping. Pour in a mold and chill until firm. 6 servings.

Mrs. R. F. Schwagel, Boonsboro, Maryland

BLACK WALNUT PUFFS
Quickly prepared; 12 minutes baking time

6 eggs, separated	2 tsp. soda
2 1-lb. packages brown sugar	6 c. flour
	2 c. chopped black walnuts

Beat the egg whites in a bowl until stiff. Beat the egg yolks in a bowl until lemon colored and fold into egg whites. Add sugar gradually and beat until light and thick. Mix the soda and flour and fold into egg mixture. Fold in walnuts and drop by spoonfuls onto a greased cookie sheet. Bake in 375-degree oven for 10 to 12 minutes. Do not overbake.

Mrs. Laura Crockett, West Palm Beach, Florida

CHEWY SQUARES
Quickly prepared; bake for 20 minutes

1 stick margarine	1 tsp. vanilla
1 box brown sugar	2 c. flour
2 eggs	1 c. broken pecans

Melt the margarine in a saucepan over low heat. Remove from heat and add the brown sugar. Add the eggs, one at a time and beat well. Add the vanilla and flour and mix with a spoon, then add the pecans. Spread in a greased 9 x 13-inch pan. Bake at 350 degrees for 20 minutes. Do not overbake.

Mrs. Jacquette K. Robinson, Glenwood, North Carolina

COOKIE KISSES
Easily prepared; allow 40 minutes to bake

2 egg whites	**1 tsp. vanilla**
1 c. light brown sugar	**2 c. chopped nuts**
2 tbsp. flour	

Beat the egg whites until stiff, then add the brown sugar and flour gradually. Add the vanilla and fold in the nuts. Drop by spoonfuls, several inches apart, on a greased pan. Bake at 250 degrees for about 35 to 40 minutes.

Katherine M. Simons, Cross, South Carolina

GOLD RUSH BROWNIES
Quickly prepared; 30 minutes baking time

1 1/2 c. graham cracker crumbs	**1 tsp. vanilla**
1 can sweetened condensed milk	**1 c. nuts**
1 6-oz. package chocolate chips	

Butter and flour an 8-inch square baking dish. Mix all the ingredients and spread in the prepared dish. Bake for 25 to 30 minutes at 325 to 350 degrees. Cut into squares. 16 brownies.

Mrs. Billie Robinson, North Little Rock, Arkansas

NO-BAKE PEANUT BUTTER COOKIES
Emergency shelf ingredients; heat and mix, then ready to serve

1/2 c. light corn syrup	**1 c. peanut butter**
1/2 c. sugar	**2 c. high protein cereal**

Bring the syrup and sugar to boil in a saucepan. Remove from heat and stir in the peanut butter and cereal. Drop by spoonfuls on metal tray or waxed paper and cool.

Mrs. Robert L. Abney, Jr., Bay Springs, Mississippi

RASPBERRY DELIGHT
Easily prepared; keep frozen until serving time

3 pt. frozen dessert topping	**2 pt. raspberry sherbet**
1 3/4 pkg. macaroons, crumbled	

Mix the dessert topping and macaroon crumbs and spread half the mixture in a 9 x 13-inch pan, then freeze. Spread the raspberry sherbet over the macaroon mixture in pan and cover with remaining crumb mixture. Freeze. May be kept indefinitely. 12-14 servings.

Mrs. W. M. Pitts, Asheboro, North Carolina

Banana Split (below)

BANANA SPLIT
Ready to prepare and serve at any time

Fresh bananas	Crushed pineapple
Strawberry ice cream	Chopped nuts
Marble ice cream	Maraschino cherries
Lemon ice cream	Chocolate syrup

Slice the bananas in thirds lengthwise. Place 3 slices in a banana split dish. Place scoops of the strawberry, marble and lemon ice creams over the banana slices. Top the strawberry ice cream with a spoonful of crushed pineapple, the marble ice cream with nuts and a cherry and the lemon ice cream with chocolate syrup.

STRAWBERRY THICKSHAKES FROM CALIFORNIA
May be prepared at least 1 hour ahead and frozen until serving time

2 pt. fresh California strawberries	1 qt. vanilla ice cream, softened

Reserve a few strawberries for garnish and puree remaining strawberries in a blender. Strain the puree through double thickness of cheesecloth to remove seeds. Blend the puree and ice cream in the blender until smooth. Place the blender container in the freezer for about 1 hour. Blend for several seconds until smooth before serving. Spoon into tall glasses and serve immediately with long spoons. Garnish with whole strawberries. 4 servings.

HOMEMADE STRAWBERRY ICE CREAM
No cooking required; may be prepared hours ahead

2 c. mashed strawberries	1 c. fresh orange juice, strained
3 c. sugar	

Juice of 1 lemon, strained   1 c. milk
1 pt. whipping cream, whipped

Combine the strawberries and sugar, then add the juices. Combine the whipped cream and milk and stir into the fruit mixture. Pour into freezer trays. Freeze till almost firm and stir, then freeze till firm. Garnish with whole strawberries to serve, if desired. 10 servings.

Mrs. A. C. Reynolds, Charlotte, North Carolina

MOCHA MOUSSE
Prepare ahead; ready to serve instantly

8 oz. semisweet chocolate   1 c. heavy cream
3 tbsp. strong coffee   3 tbsp. sugar
4 tbsp. creme de cacao

Combine the chocolate, coffee and creme de cacao in a double boiler and melt, stirring to blend, then cool. Whip the cream with the sugar until stiff. Fold the chocolate mixture into the whipped cream. Pour into a mold or paper muffin cups and freeze. Remove from freezer 10 minutes before serving, if molded. 8-10 servings.

Mrs. Truman Clark, Beaufort, South Carolina

FROZEN LEMON MOUSSE
Prepared and frozen in less than 30 minutes

2 env. unflavored gelatin   Yellow food coloring
1 6-oz. can frozen lemonade,   1 qt. vanilla ice cream
  thawed

Sprinkle the gelatin over the undiluted lemonade to soften in a small saucepan. Stir over low heat until the gelatin is dissolved. Remove from heat and stir in a few drops of food coloring. Cut the ice cream into chunks and place in a large bowl. Beat with electric mixer at medium speed just until softened. Pour the lemonade mixture into the ice cream and beat at medium speed just until blended. Turn into 4 or 5-cup mold. Refrigerate for 15 minutes or until set. Unmold onto serving plate. Garnish with thin slices of lemon, if desired.

Mrs. Chester Dalton, Oakland, Maryland

PEACH CLOUD
No cooking necessary; may be prepared hours ahead

1 c. finely chopped fresh   1 c. whipping cream, whipped
  peaches   Dash of salt
6 tbsp. sugar   2 egg whites

Mix the peaches and 1/4 cup sugar and fold into whipped cream. Add salt to egg whites and beat until soft peaks form, adding remaining sugar gradually. Fold into cream mixture and pour into molds. Freeze until firm. 6-8 servings.

Mrs. Agnes Hackley, Louisville, Kentucky

ORANGE FLAMBE
Preparation and cooking time less than 30 minutes

1/3 c. cornstarch	1 1/2 oz. Grand Marnier
2 c. mandarin orange segments with juice	1 pt. orange sherbet
	4 tsp. grain alcohol

Combine the cornstarch and 1/4 cup cold water and stir until smooth. Pour the orange segments and juice in a saucepan and bring to a boil. Stir in the cornstarch mixture and cook until thickened. Add the Grand Marnier and cool. Spoon the orange sherbet into serving dishes and top with orange sauce. Pour 1 teaspoon grain alcohol over each serving, then ignite and serve flaming.

Mrs. Andrew P. Rollins, El Paso, Texas

TORTONI WITH STRAWBERRY SAUCE
Partially prepared ahead; final preparations in 15 minutes

1 pt. vanilla ice cream	2 tbsp. chopped toasted almonds
12 macaroons, crumbled	1 pt. fresh strawberries
1/2 c. orange juice	Sugar to taste
1/2 c. heavy cream	
1 tsp. powdered sugar	

Soften the ice cream slightly and place in a bowl. Stir in the macaroons and half the orange juice. Whip the heavy cream until thick and fold into ice cream mixture. Spoon into a 3-cup mold and sprinkle with powdered sugar and almonds. Cover with plastic wrap and freeze until firm. Hull and slice the strawberries and place in a saucepan. Stir in the sugar and simmer until soft. Remove from heat and add remaining orange juice. Pour into a chafing dish. Unmold the ice cream mixture and place on a cold serving plate. Serve with strawberry sauce. One 10-ounce package frozen sliced strawberries, thawed, may be substituted for fresh strawberries.

Mrs. H. F. Norcross, Tyronza, Arkansas

CRUNCHY PEACHES AND CREAM
Preparation and cooking time less than 30 minutes

1 No. 2 1/2 can peaches	1/2 c. crumbled cornflakes
1 c. peach preserves	1 tsp. cinnamon
Brandy	1 qt. vanilla ice cream
1/2 c. brown sugar	

Drain the peaches and reserve 1/2 cup juice. Place the peaches in a 9 x 9-inch casserole. Mix the reserved juice with the peach preserves and 1 tablespoon brandy and pour over the peaches. Mix the sugar, cornflakes and cinnamon and sprinkle over the peaches. Bake for 15 minutes at 375 degrees. Place hard-frozen ice cream in 6 individual dishes and spoon the peach mix over the top. Spoon 1/2 teaspoon brandy over the finished dessert. Ignite and serve flaming for a really festive look.

Mrs. Gene Dow, Austin, Texas

GARDELLA SPECIAL
Fancy, yet easy to prepare; no cooking required

1/2 gal. vanilla ice cream	1 bottle port
1 No. 2 1/2 can fruit cocktail, drained	8 to 10 maraschino cherries

Place 1 or 2 scoops vanilla ice cream in each dessert or parfait glass and top with 2 tablespoons fruit cocktail. Pour 2 tablespoons port over the fruit. Top with maraschino cherry.

Mrs. John K. Gardella, Pensacola, Florida

PEACH MELBAS FLAMBE
Elegant but quickly prepared; 20 minutes for cooking

1 10-oz. package frozen strawberries	1 1-lb. can cling peach halves
1/4 c. currant jelly	1/4 c. slivered blanched almonds
1/4 c. undiluted frozen orange juice	3 tbsp. brandy
	1 qt. firm vanilla ice cream

Thaw the strawberries and puree in a blender or press through a sieve. Melt the jelly in a saucepan or chafing dish, then add the pureed strawberries and orange juice and heat slowly. Drain the peaches and place in the strawberry sauce over low heat. Sprinkle with the almonds. Warm the brandy, then pour over the peaches and set afire, spooning over peaches as brandy burns. Spoon a peach half into each serving dish. Top with ice cream and spoon strawberry sauce over all. 6 servings.

Peach Melbas Flambe (above)

Cherry-Nut Pudding Jubilee (below)

CHERRY-NUT PUDDING JUBILEE
May be prepared ahead and chilled until serving time

12 chocolate wafer cookies
1   15 1/2-oz. can French
   vanilla pudding
1/4 c. sour cream

1/4 c. chopped walnuts
2 tbsp. quartered maraschino
   cherries

Place 1 cookie in each of 4 individual tart pans or dessert dishes and arrange 4 cookie halves around sides. Blend the pudding and sour cream and stir in the nuts and cherries. Spoon the pudding into cookie-lined dishes. Chill, if desired. 4 servings.

BREAD PUDDING
Preparation and cooking time about 1 hour

2 tbsp. butter
2 c. hot milk
2 eggs, beaten
1/2 c. brown sugar

2 tbsp. syrup
1 tsp. vanilla
Dash of salt
1 c. bread crumbs

Stir the butter and hot milk together until melted, then pour a small portion of the hot mixture over the eggs. Return to hot mixture and add the sugar, syrup, vanilla and salt, mixing well. Pour over the bread crumbs in a buttered casserole. Bake at 325 degrees until inserted knife comes out clean. 4 servings.

Mrs. Louise Fuller, Louisville, Kentucky

APPLE PUDDING
Preparation and cooking time less than 1 hour

1/2 c. soft margarine
1 c. (packed) brown sugar

1 egg, beaten
1 c. flour

1 tsp. soda	1/2 tsp. cinnamon
1/4 tsp. salt	2 c. chopped apples
1/4 tsp. nutmeg	1 tsp. vanilla
1/2 tsp. cloves	3/4 c. chopped pecans

Cream the margarine and brown sugar in a bowl. Add the egg and mix well. Sift dry ingredients together. Add to creamed mixture and blend well. Add the apples and vanilla and mix. Pour into a greased baking dish and place pecans on top. Bake at 350 degrees for 30 to 40 minutes.

Mrs. Grady Astrop, Bristol, Virginia

BROWN SUGAR PUDDING
Quickly prepared; 25 minutes cooking time

1 c. brown sugar	1/2 c. sugar
2 c. boiling water	2 tsp. baking powder
2 tbsp. butter	1/2 c. raisins
1 c. sifted flour	1/2 c. milk

Preheat oven to 375 degrees. Combine the brown sugar, boiling water and butter in a 2-quart casserole. Place in the oven to heat while mixing batter. Sift flour, sugar and baking powder together, then add the raisins and milk. Mix thoroughly, but do not beat. Remove the casserole from the oven. Drop the batter into the syrup by spoonfuls. Bake for 20 to 25 minutes. 4 servings.

Mrs. Donald J. Cole, Columbus, Georgia

RUM-SAUCED DATE BREAD
Prepare ahead; final preparation 5 minutes

1 c. sugar	1 egg
1 c. chopped nuts	2 tbsp. flour
1 c. chopped dates	1 tbsp. baking powder
1 c. bread crumbs	2 tbsp. melted butter
1 c. milk	

Mix all ingredients thoroughly and place in a greased loaf pan. Bake for 30 minutes at 350 degrees. Cool and slice.

Rum Sauce

2 tbsp. cornstarch	2 tbsp. butter
1/2 tsp. salt	1 tsp. rum
1 c. sugar	Juice of 1/2 lemon
2 c. boiling water	

Mix the cornstarch, salt and sugar in blazer pan of chafing dish. Add the boiling water gradually, stirring constantly, and bring to a boil. Cook for 5 minutes. Add butter, rum and lemon juice and place over hot water. Serve over date bread.

Mrs. J. E. Thagard, Eufaula, Alabama

Colonial Strawberries with Quince Cream (below)

COLONIAL STRAWBERRIES WITH QUINCE CREAM
Prepare ahead; chill until serving time

> 1/4 c. quince jelly
> 1 tbsp. confectioners' sugar
> 1 c. heavy cream

> 2 pt. fresh California
> strawberries, sliced

Beat the jelly and sugar together until blended, then add the cream and beat until stiff. Chill and serve with the strawberries. 6 servings.

FRUIT COMPOTE
Prepare the fruits ahead and chill; assemble at serving time

> 2 c. watermelon balls
> 2 red unpeeled apples, cut in
> thin wedges
> 1 cantaloupe, sliced in wedges

> 2 c. grapefruit sections
> 2 bananas, sliced diagonally
> 1 6-oz. can frozen orange
> juice

Place the watermelon balls in the center of a compote. Arrange the remaining fruit around the watermelon. Spoon the orange juice over the fruit. Serve chilled. 6 servings.

Photograph for this recipe on page 2.

SHERRIED FRUIT COMPOTE
Preparation and cooking time about 30 minutes

> 5 egg yolks
> 1 c. sugar
> 1 c. cream

> 1 c. powdered sugar
> 1/2 c. sherry
> 3 pt. fresh fruit cubes

Break the egg yolks in the top of a double boiler and stir in the sugar, cream and powdered sugar. Cook over hot water until slightly thickened. Add the sherry, stirring to blend, then cool. Place the fruit in compote and pour the sherry sauce over the fruit.

Mrs. Martha Jo Michie, Birmingham, Alabama

FIGS WITH HONEY AND CREAM
Prepare ahead; chill until serving time

1 qt. fresh figs, stems removed	1/3 c. honey
1 pt. white wine	1 pt. heavy cream

Wash the figs and place in a saucepan. Mix the wine and honey and pour over figs. Bring to boiling point and reduce heat. Simmer for 5 minutes and chill. Serve with cream. 4-6 servings.

Mrs. W. M. Smith, Prattville, Alabama

CHEESECAKE
Easily prepared; allow 1 hour for baking

3 8-oz. packages cream cheese	5 eggs
1 c. sugar	Graham cracker crust
1 tsp. vanilla	

Let the cream cheese stand at room temperature until soft, then place in a large mixing bowl with the sugar and vanilla. Beat with electric mixer until slightly blended. Beat in eggs, one at a time, until smooth. Pour over graham cracker crust in 9 x 13-inch pan. Bake at 375 degrees for about 1 hour or until toothpick inserted in cake comes out clean. 20 servings.

Mrs. Thomas Spear, Anniston, Alabama

DIETER'S CHEESECAKE
Prepare ahead; chill until serving time

2 env. unflavored gelatin	1 1/2 tsp. vanilla
1 c. liquified nonfat dry milk	1/2 tsp. almond extract
4 eggs, separated	3 c. low-calorie cottage cheese
1 1/4 c. sugar substitute	1/2 tsp. cream of tartar
1/4 tsp. salt	1/3 c. graham cracker crumbs
1 tsp. grated lemon rind	1/8 tsp. cinnamon
1 tbsp. lemon juice	1/8 tsp. nutmeg

Sprinkle the gelatin over the milk in the top of a double boiler. Add the egg yolks and stir until blended. Cook and stir over hot water for about 5 minutes or until gelatin dissolves and mixture thickens slightly. Remove from heat and stir in sugar substitute, salt, grated rind, lemon juice and flavorings. Sieve or beat the cottage cheese with electric mixer at high speed until smooth, then stir into the gelatin mixture. Chill, stirring occasionally, until mixture mounds slightly when dropped from a spoon. Beat the egg whites and cream of tartar together until stiff and fold into the gelatin mixture. Combine the graham cracker crumbs, cinnamon and nutmeg and sprinkle about half the crumbs into a 9-inch spring-form pan. Turn the gelatin mixture into the pan over the crumb mixture and sprinkle with the remaining crumb mixture. Chill until firm. Loosen from side of pan with sharp knife, then remove side of pan. 12 servings.

Mrs. Mildred Buck, Thomaston, Alabama

Bowl-Over Apple Pie (below)

BOWL-OVER APPLE PIE
Preparation and cooking time about 30 minutes

5 c. canned apple slices	2 tbsp. butter or margarine
3/4 c. (firmly packed) brown	1 tbsp. grated lemon rind
sugar	Pastry for 1-crust pie
Dash of salt	Nutmeg

Combine the apple slices, 1/2 cup water, brown sugar, salt, butter and lemon rind in a saucepan and cook over moderate heat until hot and thickened. Roll out the pastry into a 12-inch round and prick all over. Place a round bottomed heatproof bowl or casserole upside down on a cookie sheet and press pastry lightly to bowl and turn back overhang flush with edge of bowl to make a double edge flute. Bake the crust at 400 degrees for about 12 to 14 minutes or until browned and crisp. Cool for several minutes, then lift the pastry crust carefully from the bowl and place like a bowl on a serving dish. Spoon the hot apple filling into crust and sprinkle generously with nutmeg. Serve at once with whipped cream. 6-8 servings.

CHOCOLATE CANDY BAR ICE BOX PIE
Prepare ahead; chill until serving time

9 chocolate candy bars	Vanilla to taste
1/2 c. cream	1 c. pecans
1 10-oz. package marshmallows	2 9-in. baked pie shells
2 1/2 c. whipped cream	Grated chocolate
Sugar to taste	

Place the candy, cream and marshmallows in a saucepan and heat, stirring until melted. Remove from heat and cool to room temperature. Fold the whipped cream, sugar and vanilla together, then fold 1 1/2 cups whipped cream and the pecans into the chocolate mixture. Pour into the cooled pie shells and top with 1 cup whipped cream. Sprinkle the chocolate on top and refrigerate. 16 servings.

Mrs. James C. Snell, Newport News, Virginia

APRICOT PIE
Prepare ahead, chill until serving time

1 No. 303 can apricot halves	1/2 pt. whipped cream
1 can sweetened condensed milk	Wafers
1/4 c. lemon juice	

Drain and mash the apricots. Combine the milk, lemon juice, apricots and 4 tablespoons whipped cream. Line a 9-inch pie pan with wafers and add the apricot filling. Top with remaining whipped cream and chill. 6 servings.

Mrs. Jane Ellison, Penelope, Texas

MACAROON PIE
Elegant but quickly prepared; about 30 minutes for cooking

3 egg whites	12 chopped dates
3/4 c. sugar	1/2 c. chopped nuts
1 tsp. almond flavoring	Whipped cream or topping
12 saltine crackers, crushed	

Beat the egg whites until soft peaks form then add the sugar gradually, beating until stiff. Add the flavoring and fold in the crumbs, dates and nuts. Turn into a greased 10-inch pie pan and bake for 30 to 35 minutes at 325 degrees. Serve with whipped cream or whipped topping. 6-8 servings.

Mrs. Virginia Sims, Montgomery, Alabama

RASPBERRY CHIFFON PIE
Prepare ahead; chill until serving time

1 10-oz. package frozen red raspberries, thawed	1 env. dessert topping mix
	Dash of salt
1 3-oz. package raspberry gelatin	2 egg whites
	1/4 c. sugar
3/4 c. boiling water	1 baked 9-in. pastry shell
2 tbsp. lemon juice	

Drain the raspberries and add enough water to raspberry syrup to make 2/3 cup liquid. Dissolve the gelatin in boiling water and add the lemon juice and raspberry syrup. Chill until partially set, then beat until soft peaks form. Prepare the dessert topping according to package directions, then fold the raspberries and half the topping into the gelatin mixture. Add the salt to the egg whites and beat until soft peaks form. Add the sugar gradually and beat to stiff peaks. Fold in the raspberry mixture. Pile into cooled pastry shell and chill. Spoon remaining whipped topping mix into a pastry bag or press. Form scrolls on top of chilled pie. Whole fresh or frozen raspberries may be placed on top of pie for additional garnish. 7-8 servings.

Mrs. Jack Stodghill, Temple Terrace, Florida

CHOCOLATE FUDGE
Preparation and cooking time less than 30 minutes

4 1/2 c. sugar	2 6-oz. packages chocolate chips
1 lge. can evaporated milk	1 sq. unsweetened chocolate
1/3 c. butter	1 tsp. vanilla
1 8-oz. jar marshmallow creme	1 c. nuts

Boil the sugar, milk and butter in a saucepan until mixture reaches the soft-ball stage. Remove from heat and add marshmallow creme and chocolate. Beat until smooth and chocolate is blended. Add the vanilla and nuts and mix well. Pour into a buttered pan and cool. Cut into desired pieces. 2 pounds.

Mrs. G. C. Hughes, Bartlesville, Oklahoma

FESTIVE FUDGE
Prepare ahead; may be stored for days

1 pkg. lime gelatin	1/4 c. butter
3 1/2 c. sugar	4 sq. melted semisweet chocolate
1/4 tsp. soda	Chopped nuts
1 1/2 c. milk	

Combine gelatin, sugar, soda and milk in a large saucepan and cook over medium heat, stirring until dissolved. Continue cooking, without stirring to a soft-ball stage. Remove from heat and add the butter. Cool to lukewarm, then beat until thick. Pour into an 8 x 8-inch pan. Spread the chocolate over the top and sprinkle with nuts. Cut into 1-inch squares. Keep in a cool place. Fudge improves with age.

Mrs. Greg Harden, Greenville, South Carolina

HAYSTACKS
Prepare ahead; may be stored for several days

2 pkg. butterscotch morsels	1 c. chopped peanuts
1 3-oz. can chow mein noodles	

Melt the butterscotch morsels in the top of a double boiler over low heat, then stir in the noodles and peanuts. Drop onto waxed paper and let stand until firm.

Lorna Hinson, Hickory Grove, South Carolina

PEANUT BUTTER BALLS
Prepare ahead; chill until serving time

1 1/4 lb. confectioners' sugar	1/2 lb. peanut butter
1/2 lb. margarine	1/2 lb. marshmallow creme

Mix half the sugar with the margarine. Add the peanut butter and marshmallow creme and mix well. Add the remaining sugar and shape into balls. Roll balls in sugar, if desired. Refrigerate. 2 1/2 pounds.

Mrs. Larry Gantt, Jackson, Mississippi

HONEY BALLS
Mix and stir; ready to serve

1 c. peanut butter	1 tsp. vanilla
1 c. honey	1/2 c. wheat germ
2 c. instant nonfat dry milk	

Mix the peanut butter and honey in a bowl. Add the milk and mix thoroughly. Stir in the vanilla and wheat germ and shape into small balls. Roll in additional wheat germ. 50 balls.

Augusta Richardson, Stratford, Oklahoma

NO-COOK FONDANT
Partially prepared ahead and chilled; final preparation in several minutes

1/2 c. butter	2/3 c. sweetened condensed milk
1 tsp. vanilla	6 c. confectioners' sugar, sifted
1 tsp. salt	Melted sweetened chocolate

Combine the butter, vanilla, salt and milk in a bowl and beat with electric mixer for 10 minutes. Stir in 3 cups sugar. Knead in remaining sugar. Form into eggs and refrigerate overnight. Coat with chocolate and garnish with frosting in cake decorator. 12 small eggs.

Mrs. C. M. Roache, Houston, Texas

PARTY LOGS
Easily prepared; may be stored days ahead

1 c. brown sugar	1 c. chopped pecans
1/2 c. butter	1/2 c. shredded coconut
1 c. chopped dates	2 c. oven-toasted rice cereal

Boil the brown sugar, butter and dates together in a saucepan for 5 minutes. Remove from heat and add the pecans, coconut and cereal. Cool until mixture can be handled. Shape into small logs. 2 1/2 dozen.

Mrs. Cecelia Crossett, Burna, Kentucky

SPICY SUGARED NUTS
Easily prepared in less than 30 minutes

1 c. sugar	1/2 tsp. ground cloves
1 tsp. salt	1/2 c. water
2 tsp. cinnamon	2 c. pecan halves

Combine first 5 ingredients in a saucepan and cook to soft-ball stage. Remove from heat. Add the pecans and stir until creamy. Turn out onto waxed paper. Separate pecans and cool. Other nuts may be substituted for pecans.

Mrs. Raymond Collins, Wilmington, Delaware

Spicy Fig Loaf (page 185)

breads

What southern-style recipe collection would be complete without its full array of breads? Bread-baking is an art, and southern women take understandable pride in their mastery of that art. Perhaps that's why breads ranging from just-baked yeast bread to flavorful corn bread are featured in almost every southern home.

You might consider bread-baking too time-consuming to be anything but a culinary luxury. But you need feel that way no longer with the recipes awaiting you in these pages. The next time chicken or ham makes its appearance on your dinner table, complement it by featuring Heirloom Sweet Potato Biscuits. One bite, and you're sure to discover why biscuits have long been cherished by Southerners.

The entire wonderful spectrum of breads is on parade in this section. Browse through the pages, and imagine your family's delight when you serve them Quick Bread Sticks . . . tender, moist Oatmeal Muffins . . . Parker House Rolls . . . every bread for every kind of meal.

Best of all, these home-tested recipes have had their preparation times pared down to the minimum. You won't have to spend hours in the kitchen in order to give your family the incomparable taste treat of home-baked breads. Just take a few minutes, one of these recipes, and then get ready for smiles of approval from everyone around your dining table!

173

BLUE CHEESE BISCUITS
Preparation and baking time less than 30 minutes

1 pkg. refrigerator biscuits	**3 tbsp. crumbled blue cheese**
1/4 c. butter or margarine	

Cut the biscuits in quarters and place in 2 greased 8-inch round layer pans. Melt the butter and cheese in a saucepan and spoon over biscuit pieces, being sure to coat all. Bake at 400 degrees for 15 minutes or until golden brown. Serve hot.

Miriam Calvert, Brandon, Mississippi

CHEESE BISCUITS
Partially prepared ahead and chilled; 10 minutes to bake

1 lb. sharp Cheddar cheese, grated	**1/2 tsp. salt**
2 c. butter	**1 egg, beaten**
4 c. self-rising flour	**Nut halves**

Cream the cheese and butter together until smooth. Sift flour and salt together and add to the cheese mixture. Refrigerate until chilled. Roll out a small amount at a time to 1/4-inch thickness between sheets of floured waxed paper. Cut with a small biscuit cutter and place on lightly greased cookie sheet. Brush with egg, and place a nut half on each biscuit. Bake in 375-degree oven for about 10 minutes. Do not brown. 100 biscuits.

Mrs. L. T. Southall, Quinton, Virginia

HEIRLOOM SWEET POTATO BISCUITS
Quick leftovers dividend; 15 minutes cooking time

2 c. flour	**1/2 c. shortening**
2/3 c. sugar	**2 c. mashed baked sweet**
2 tbsp. baking powder	**potatoes**
1 1/2 tsp. salt	**1/4 c. milk**

Sift the flour, sugar, baking powder and salt together and cut in the shortening until mixture is cornmeal consistency. Mix in the sweet potatoes and add milk to make a soft dough. Turn out on lightly floured board and knead lightly. Roll to 1/2-inch thickness and cut with a biscuit cutter. Place on a greased cookie sheet. Bake at 475 degrees for 12 to 15 minutes. 2 dozen biscuits.

Mrs. Alta P. Addis, Gaffney, South Carolina

PARMESAN BISCUITS
Quickly prepared; 20 minutes baking time

1 clove of garlic, minced	**2 pkg. refrigerator biscuits**
1/4 c. melted butter or margarine	**1/4 c. grated Parmesan cheese**

Mix the garlic and butter and dip biscuits in butter mixture. Overlap 13 biscuits around outer edge of 9 x 1 1/2-inch round cake pan. Overlap remaining biscuits in center. Drizzle remaining butter over top and sprinkle with cheese. Bake at 425 degrees for 15 to 20 minutes.

Mrs. M. A. Forester, Jackson, Mississippi

QUICK BREADSTICKS
Quickly prepared; 10 minutes baking time

1 can refrigerator biscuits	2 tbsp. caraway or poppy seed
1 1/2 c. crushed oven toasted	2 tsp. seasoned salt
rice cereal	1/3 c. milk

Cut each biscuit in half, then pull each half to a 4-inch length and shape like a breadstick. Combine the cereal, seed and seasoned salt. Dip the sticks in the milk and roll in crumb mixture. Place on a greased cookie sheet. Bake at 450 degrees for 10 minutes. 20 sticks.

Mrs. J. M. Boyd, Enterprise, Alabama

QUICK ONION BISCUITS
Quickly prepared; 10 minutes baking time

2 tbsp. instant minced onion	1 pkg. refrigerator biscuits
2 tbsp. melted butter	

Mix the onion and butter. Place the biscuits on an ungreased baking sheet. Press with bottom of small glass dipped in flour to make a hollow in center of each biscuit and fill with butter mixture. Bake at 450 degrees for 8 to 10 minutes or until brown. 10 biscuits

Mrs. James R. Betts, Dade City, Florida

ROSEMARY BISCUITS
Easily prepared and baked in about 20 minutes

2 c. self-rising flour	1/4 c. shortening
1 tsp. rosemary	3/4 c. milk

Place the flour and rosemary in a mixing bowl and cut in the shortening. Add the milk and blend with a spoon. Drop into greased muffin pan. Bake in 475-degree oven for 12 to 15 minutes. 12 servings.

Mrs. Etna Gaskin, Wewahitchka, Florida

BUBBLY CHEESE TOAST
Prepared and ready to serve in 10 minutes

9 slices whole wheat bread	Sharp Cheddar cheese

Cut each bread slice into 4 pieces. Cut a cheese slice to fit each bread piece and place on a baking sheet. Broil until the cheese is bubbly and lightly browned. 6 servings.

Mrs. Betty Johnson, Mobile, Alabama

Herb Bread (below)

HERB BREAD
May be prepared ahead and stored until serving time

2 c. milk	7 to 7 1/2 c. sifted
2 tsp. herb seasoning	all-purpose flour
4 tsp. caraway seed	1 tbsp. salt
1 tsp. aniseed	1/3 c. soft shortening
1/4 c. sugar	3 eggs
2 pkg. granular yeast	

Measure the milk into a saucepan, then add the herb seasoning, caraway seed and aniseed and heat to the boiling point. Pour into a mixing bowl, then add the sugar and cool to lukewarm. Soften the yeast in 1/4 cup warm water and add to the milk mixture. Add 3 cups flour and beat thoroughly, then add salt and shortening. Add the eggs, one at a time, beating well after each addition. Beat in as much of remaining flour as possible, then stir in with a spoon until the dough begins to leave sides of the bowl. Turn out on a floured board and knead until smooth and satiny. Place in a greased bowl and cover, then let rise in a warm place until doubled in bulk. Divide into 2 equal portions and form each into a loaf. Place each in a greased baking pan. Let rise until doubled in bulk. Bake in 375-degree oven for 40 to 50 minutes or until done. Remove from pans immediately and cool on a rack away from drafts.

GARLIC BREAD
Easily prepared; allow 25 minutes to bake

1 loaf Italian bread	2 tsp. garlic powder
1/4 lb. butter, melted	

Cut the bread into slices without cutting through bottom. Mix the butter and garlic powder and spread with pastry brush on both sides of each slice of bread. Wrap in foil. Bake in 350-degree oven for 25 minutes. 6 servings.

Mrs. Christine Baker, Lancaster, South Carolina

TOASTED CHEESE BREAD
Quickly prepared; baking time 10 minutes

1 loaf unsliced bread	**Grated Parmesan cheese**
Soft butter	

Remove all except the bottom crust from the loaf of bread. Slice crosswise at 1/2-inch intervals down to, but not through, the bottom crust. Spread all surfaces generously with the butter and sprinkle with cheese. Place on a cookie sheet. Bake at 350 degrees for about 10 minutes or until browned.

Mrs. Curtis Parker, Tulsa, Oklahoma

EGG BREAD
Quickly prepared; 15 minutes cooking time

1/2 c. butter	**1/2 c. milk**
1/2 loaf stale bread, cut into	**1/2 tsp. salt**
cubes	**1/2 tsp. pepper**
3 eggs, beaten	

Melt the butter in a large skillet over low heat and toss the bread cubes in the butter until lightly browned. Mix the eggs, milk, salt and pepper and pour over the bread cubes. Cook over medium heat until egg mixture is set and browned on the bottom. Serve immediately. 6 servings.

Mrs. Edna Womer, Chester, West Virginia

CREAM OF WHEAT BREAD
Easily prepared; allow 30 minutes for cooking

1 c. cream of wheat, uncooked	**1/2 tsp. salt**
1 c. flour	**1 c. milk**
1/4 c. sugar	**1/4 c. cooking oil**
4 tsp. baking powder	**1 egg**

Mix the first 5 ingredients well and add the milk, oil and egg. Stir gently until blended. Place in a greased pan. Bake at 425 degrees until top is golden brown. 4 servings.

Mrs. L. C. Kirkland, Walnut Ridge, Arkansas

PICCALILLI HOT BREAD
Quickly prepared; 20 minutes baking time

2 c. biscuit mix	**1 tbsp. oil**
2/3 c. milk	**1/3 c. drained sweet pickle**
1 egg, slightly beaten	**relish**
2 tbsp. instant minced onion	**1/4 c. grated Parmesan cheese**

Measure the biscuit mix into a large bowl. Combine the milk, egg, onion, oil and relish and add all at once to the dry mixture. Stir until just moistened. Turn into a greased 8-inch pan and sprinkle with the cheese. Bake in 400-degree oven for 17 to 20 minutes or until the bread is done and cheese is golden. Serve hot. 6-8 servings.

Mrs. B. T. Fowler, Hot Springs, Arkansas

HERBED FRENCH BREAD
Quickly prepared; 15 minutes baking time

1 c. soft butter	1/2 tsp. savory
1/2 tsp. marjoram	1/2 tsp. paprika
1/2 tsp. thyme	1/4 tsp. cayenne pepper
1/2 tsp. oregano	1 loaf French bread, sliced

Mix the butter and seasonings together thoroughly and spread on both sides of bread slices. Wrap in foil. Bake for 15 minutes at 350 degrees.

Mrs. Loretta Kersey, Williamsburg, Kentucky

HOT SESAME BREAD
Easily prepared; 30 minutes baking time

2 cans refrigerator biscuits	Sesame seed
1 egg white, slightly beaten	

Preheat oven to 350 degrees. Open biscuits according to package directions but do not separate. Place rolls of biscuits, end to end, on a cookie sheet. Press together lightly, shaping ends to form a long loaf. Brush with egg white and sprinkle with sesame seed. Bake for 30 minutes or until a rich golden brown. 1 loaf.

Marilyn Berousek, Maysville, Oklahoma

BARBECUE BREAD
Quickly prepared; ready to serve in 20 minutes

1 round loaf pumpernickel bread	2 tbsp. mustard
1 stick soft butter	1/4 c. snipped parsley

Cut the bread into 1/2-inch slices. Mix remaining ingredients and spread over the slices. Press the loaf together on a large piece of foil. Cut the bread in half lengthwise almost to bottom crust. Bring edges of the foil over loaf to cover. Heat at side of grill for 20 to 25 minutes or until hot, turning occasionally. May also be warmed in oven.

Mrs. Quentin Pitts, Goldsboro, North Carolina

SALLY LUNN
Easily prepared in several minutes; 25 minutes to bake

1/2 c. shortening	1/4 tsp. salt
1/4 c. sugar	1 c. milk
4 tsp. baking powder	3 eggs, beaten
2 c. flour	

Cream the shortening with the sugar. Mix and sift the dry ingredients together, then add to the creamed mixture, alternating with the milk. Add the eggs and mix well. Pour into a loaf pan. Bake at 400 degrees for 25 minutes. Break the bread into squares to serve. 6 servings.

Mrs. Jack A. Derby, Fort Worth, Texas

ONION BREAD
Preparation and cooking time about 30 minutes

1 loaf French-style bread	**1/4 lb. softened butter**
5 to 7 scallions	

Cut the loaf in half lengthwise. Chop the scallions and add to the butter, then spread on all sides of the bread halves. Wrap in aluminum foil. Bake in 400-degree oven for 20 minutes. 4-6 servings.

Mrs. Andrew Myers, Columbia, South Carolina

CRANBERRY MUFFINS
Quickly prepared; 25 minutes baking time

2 c. packaged biscuit mix	**2 tbsp. melted butter**
1/3 c. sugar	**3/4 c. whole cranberry**
3/4 c. milk	**sauce, drained**
1 egg	

Combine the biscuit mix, sugar, milk, egg and melted butter in a bowl and mix until dry ingredients are dampened. Break up the cranberry sauce with a fork and fold into the batter. Fill well-greased muffin tins 2/3 full. Bake at 400 degrees for 20 to 25 minutes. 12 muffins.

Cranberry Muffins (above)

OATMEAL MUFFINS
10 minutes to prepare; 20 minutes to bake

1 c. quick oatmeal	1 tsp. salt
1 c. buttermilk	1 tsp. baking powder
1 egg	1/2 tsp. soda
1/2 c. brown sugar	1/4 c. (about) melted fat
1 c. flour	

Combine the oatmeal and buttermilk and set aside for 5 minutes. Add the egg and sugar to the oatmeal mixture and mix well. Add the flour, salt, baking powder and soda, then add the fat and mix lightly. Pour in greased muffin tins. Bake at 400 degrees for about 20 minutes.

Mrs. William L. Bassett, Clearwater, Florida

POPOVERS
Quickly prepared; 40 minutes baking time

2 eggs, beaten	1 c. sifted all-purpose flour
1 c. milk	1/2 tsp. salt
1 tbsp. melted shortening	

Combine the eggs, milk and shortening, then add the flour and salt and beat with a rotary beater until the batter is smooth and free of lumps. Pour into hot, oiled custard cups or muffin pans, filling 1/2 full. Bake for 15 minutes at 425 degrees, then reduce oven temperature to 350 degrees and bake for about 20 minutes longer. Add 1/4 cup grated sharp Cheddar cheese, if desired. 8-12 servings.

Mrs. Marjorie West, Lauderdale, Mississippi

DELIGHTFUL CHILDREN'S BREAKFAST

Refrigerator Bran Muffins *page 180*
Eggs with Cheese *page 142*
Orange Juice

REFRIGERATOR BRAN MUFFINS
Prepare ahead; 20 minutes for baking

1 qt. buttermilk	4 eggs, beaten
2 c. boiling water	5 c. flour
5 tsp. soda	1 tbsp. salt
1 c. shortening	3 c. whole bran cereal
2 c. sugar	2 c. bran flakes

Mix the buttermilk, water and soda. Cream the shortening and sugar, then beat in the eggs. Combine remaining ingredients and add alternately with buttermilk mixture to the creamed mixture. Keep in covered container until ready for use. Nuts, raisins or dates may be added. Spoon into greased muffin tins. Bake in 400-degree oven for about 20 minutes. 5 dozen muffins.

Mrs. Carolyn Green, Jackson, Mississippi

MYSTERY MUFFINS
10 minutes to prepare; 20 minutes to bake

1 c. self-rising flour
3 tbsp. mayonnaise

1/2 c. milk

Place the flour in a bowl and add the mayonnaise and milk. Stir till blended. Fill greased muffin cups 2/3 full. Bake at 425 degrees for 16 to 20 minutes. 6 servings.

Mrs. F. M. Amman, Parris Island, South Carolina

PARSLEY ROLLS
6 minutes to prepare; 6 minutes to bake

2 tbsp. melted butter
1 tsp. lemon juice
6 brown-and-serve butterflake rolls

2 tbsp. chopped parsley
2 tsp. chopped chives

Mix the butter and lemon juice. Separate sections of rolls partially and brush between sections with half the butter mixture. Sprinkle with most of the parsley and chives. Place rolls in muffin cups and brush tops with remaining butter mixture. Sprinkle with remaining parsley and chives. Bake at 400 degrees for about 6 minutes or until brown.

Mrs. Walter Andrews, Tucson, Arizona

CORN DODGERS
Quickly prepared; 20 minutes to bake

1 c. cornmeal
1 tsp. salt
1 tbsp. bacon grease

1 1/2 tsp. sugar
1 c. boiling water
1 egg, beaten

Preheat oven to 400 degrees. Combine the cornmeal, salt, bacon grease and sugar and pour in the boiling water, then beat in the egg. Drop from teaspoon or tablespoon onto a greased cookie sheet. Bake for 15 to 20 minutes or until golden brown. 4-6 servings.

Mrs. Lawson W. Magruder, Arlington, Virginia

LOUISIANA HUSH PUPPIES
Preparation and cooking time less than 30 minutes

1 1/2 c. cornmeal
1/2 c. flour
4 green onions, chopped
1 egg, beaten
1/8 tsp. salt

2 tbsp. baking powder
1/2 tsp. soda
1 c. buttermilk
4 tbsp. melted bacon drippings

Combine all the ingredients in a large bowl and mix well. Drop by spoonfuls into hot oil in a heavy skillet or Dutch oven. Cook until golden brown.

Mrs. Robert C. Lowther, Alexandria, Louisiana

SPIDER CORN BREAD
5 minutes to prepare; 25 minutes to bake

1 1/3 c. cornmeal	2 tsp. baking powder
1/3 c. flour	2 eggs, slightly beaten
2 tbsp. sugar	2 c. milk
1 tsp. salt	3 tbsp. butter, melted

Mix the cornmeal, flour, sugar, salt and baking powder, then add the eggs, 1 cup milk and butter. Pour into pan and pour remaining milk over the batter. Do not stir. Bake for 25 minutes at 350 degrees.

Gertrude Kirk, Saluda, North Carolina

MISSISSIPPI-STYLE CORN BREAD
Easily prepared; allow about 25 minutes to bake

4 tbsp. bacon grease	4 tsp. baking powder
1 c. flour	1/4 tsp. soda
1 c. cornmeal	1 1/2 c. buttermilk
1 tsp. salt	2 lge. eggs

Preheat oven to 425 degrees. Place the bacon grease in an iron skillet. Place the skillet in hot oven while mixing the batter. Sift all the dry ingredients together and add the buttermilk, then the eggs. Stir briskly. Pour the hot bacon grease out of the skillet into the batter, then pour the batter immediately into the heated skillet. Bake for 20 to 25 minutes.

Mrs. G. L. Irwin, Alexandria, Virginia

PARKER HOUSE ROLLS
Partially prepared ahead; allow 15 minutes for baking

2 c. milk	1/4 c. lukewarm water
Sugar	2 eggs, beaten
2 tsp. salt	6 c. flour
1/4 c. shortening	Melted butter
2 env. yeast	

Mix the milk, 1/4 cup sugar, salt and shortening in a saucepan and heat to boiling point, then cool to lukewarm. Dissolve the yeast and 5 tablespoons sugar in lukewarm water, then add yeast mixture, eggs and 4 cups flour to the milk mixture. Beat well, then stir in remaining flour. Let rise for 2 to 3 hours or until doubled in size. Knead lightly, then shape in rolls. Crease with back of knife, cutting nearly through and pull almost apart. Dip top in melted butter and fold in half. Place in baking pan and let rise for about 35 minutes. Bake in 375-degree oven for 12 to 15 minutes. Brush tops with melted butter.

Mrs. S. W. Rowe, Macon, Georgia

CRESCENT ROLLS
Partially prepared ahead; allow 15 minutes for baking

1 env. yeast	4 tbsp. sugar
1/4 c. lukewarm water	1 tsp. salt
3/4 c. milk	3 eggs, beaten
1/2 c. butter	4 1/2 c. sifted flour

Soften the yeast in the water. Scald the milk and stir in the butter, sugar and salt, then cool to lukewarm. Stir in the yeast, eggs and flour and knead until a smooth dough is formed. Place in a greased bowl, then cover and let rise until doubled in bulk. Divide the dough in thirds and roll each piece into a 10-inch circle. Cut into 12 wedge-shaped pieces. Roll up each piece from the wide end to the point. Place on a greased baking pan and pull ends inward to make a crescent. Let rise until doubled in bulk, then brush with melted butter. Bake in a 400-degree oven for 15 minutes or until browned. 36 rolls.

Mrs. Clark Dunn, Baton Rouge, Louisiana

OATMEAL YEAST ROLLS
Allow 2 hours for rolls to rise; 30 minutes baking time

1 1/2 c. boiling water	1 beaten egg
1/3 c. shortening	1 env. dry yeast
1/3 c. (firmly packed) brown sugar	3/4 c. instant nonfat dry milk
1 tsp. salt	1 qt. sifted all-purpose flour
1 c. rolled oats	

Pour the boiling water into a 5-quart bowl and add the shortening, brown sugar, salt and rolled oats. Cool to lukewarm and add the egg and crumbled yeast. Sift the nonfat dry milk with 2 cups of flour and add to the oat mixture. Beat until smooth, then add remaining flour, a small amount at a time, until dough can be handled. Knead until smooth on a floured board, then place in a greased bowl. Cover with waxed paper and a towel and set in a warm place until doubled in bulk. Punch down and let dough rest for 10 minutes. Shape into 32 balls about 1 1/2 inches in diameter and place 1 inch apart in 2 well-greased 8-inch pans. Cover and let rise until doubled in bulk. Bake at 375 degrees for 25 to 30 minutes or until browned.

Oatmeal Yeast Rolls (above)

BLUEBERRY MUFFINS
Quickly prepared; 25 minutes baking time

1 1/3 c. flour	2 eggs, beaten
2 tsp. baking powder	2/3 c. milk
1/2 tsp. salt	3 tbsp. cooking oil
4 tbsp. brown sugar	2/3 c. fresh or frozen
1 tbsp. sugar	blueberries

Mix the dry ingredients together. Combine the eggs, milk and oil and add to the dry mixture, stirring only until moistened. Add the blueberries, stirring carefully, then spoon into greased muffin tins. Bake in 425-degree oven for 25 minutes. 12 muffins.

Mrs. George Grafton, Fredonia, Arizona

COTTAGE CHEESE FRUIT BREAD
Partially prepared ahead; about 1 hour for baking

2/3 c. dried apricots	1 tbsp. grated orange rind
2/3 c. dried prunes	1 1/2 c. cottage cheese
1/3 c. butter	2 c. sifted all-purpose flour
1/2 c. (firmly packed) light	2 tsp. baking powder
brown sugar	3/4 tsp. soda
2 eggs	3/4 tsp. salt
1 tbsp. grated lemon rind	

Place the apricots and prunes in a 1-quart saucepan and add water just to cover fruit. Boil over low heat, uncovered, for about 30 minutes or until all liquid is absorbed. Cool, then chop the fruits. Cream the butter and sugar in a large mixing bowl. Add the eggs, one at a time, beating well after each addition. Add the lemon and orange rinds and cottage cheese and beat well. Sift the flour, baking powder, soda and salt together, then add to creamed mixture and beat at low speed just until combined. Fold in the chopped fruits and spread into 2 well-buttered 7 1/2 x 3 3/4 x 2 1/4-inch pans. Bake in a 350-degree oven for 45 to 50 minutes. Allow to stand for 10 minutes, then remove from pan onto wire rack to cool.

Cottage Cheese Fruit Bread (above)

BUTTERSCOTCH-NUT BREAD
Easily prepared; allow 1 hour for baking

1 box brown sugar	1 tsp. salt
3 tbsp. melted shortening	2 c. sour milk
2 eggs	4 c. flour
2 tsp. soda	1/2 c. chopped nuts

Grease and flour two 4 x 8-inch loaf pans. Place all ingredients except nuts in a large bowl and mix with electric mixer at high speed for 3 minutes, then fold in the nuts. Pour into prepared pans. Bake at 325 degrees for about 1 hour. Turn out of pans and cool.

Mrs. Harold Parks, Lawton, Oklahoma

SPICY FIG LOAF
Easily prepared; allow 1 hour for baking

3 c. sifted flour	1/2 c. chopped pecans
3/4 c. sugar	3/4 c. chopped California
4 tsp. baking powder	dried figs
1 tsp. soda	1 1/2 c. quick-cooking
1 tsp. salt	oatmeal
1 tsp. cinnamon	2 c. buttermilk
1/2 tsp. ginger	1/3 c. salad oil

Sift the flour with the sugar, baking powder, soda, salt, cinnamon and ginger. Stir in the pecans, figs and oatmeal. Stir the buttermilk and oil into dry ingredients. Pour into a greased 9 x 5-inch loaf pan. Bake at 350 degrees for about 1 hour. Let stand for several minutes, then remove from pan and cool on a rack.

Photograph for this recipe on page 172.

ORANGE GINGERBREAD
20 minutes to prepare; 30 minutes to bake

1 1/2 c. sifted flour	1/2 c. sugar
3/4 tsp. soda	2 eggs
1/4 tsp. salt	2 tbsp. grated orange rind
1/2 tsp. ginger	1/2 c. dark molasses
1/2 tsp. cinnamon	1/2 c. hot coffee
1/2 c. butter or margarine	

Sift the flour, soda, salt, ginger and cinnamon together. Cream the butter and sugar in a mixing bowl. Add the eggs, one at a time, beating well after each addition. Add orange rind. Blend molasses and coffee together. Add dry ingredients to creamed mixture alternately with coffee mixture, beginning and ending with dry ingredients and beat until smooth. Pour into a greased and floured 9-inch square baking pan. Bake at 375 degrees for 25 to 30 minutes or until cake tester inserted in center comes out clean.

Mrs. Ross Gutierrez, Hurst, Texas

PEANUT BUTTER BREAD
May be prepared a day ahead; then ready to serve

2 c. sifted flour	1 egg
1 1/2 tsp. salt	2/3 c. sugar
3 tsp. baking powder	1 c. milk
1/2 tsp. cinnamon	4 tbsp. salad oil
3/4 c. peanut butter	

Preheat oven to 350 degrees. Grease a 9-inch loaf pan. Sift the flour, salt, baking powder and cinnamon together into a large bowl. Add the peanut butter, egg, sugar, milk and salad oil. Mix at medium speed for 1 minute, then turn into prepared pan. Bake at 350 degrees for 1 hour. Store for at least 1 day.

Mrs. B. H. Fulton, Laurel, Mississippi

POTATO PANCAKES
Easily prepared; 20 minutes cooking time

2 c. raw grated potatoes	1 tsp. salt
3 eggs, beaten	1 tbsp. flour
1 tbsp. cooking oil	

Mix the potatoes, eggs, oil, salt and flour together until blended. Cook 2 tablespoonfuls at a time in a hot greased frypan or on a well-greased hot griddle. Turn only once. Pancakes should be lightly browned and lacy-edged. Serve hot with syrup or applesauce.

Mrs. Elwood Henry, San Angelo, Texas

BLINCHIKI
Elegant, but quickly prepared; 20 to 30 minutes for cooking

1/4 c. flour	2 eggs, beaten
1 tbsp. sugar	Milk
1/2 tsp. baking powder	Butter

Mix the flour, sugar and baking powder in a bowl. Add the eggs and mix well. Mix in enough milk to make batter consistency of cream. Heat 8-inch skillet with 1/4 teaspoon butter. Pour enough batter in skillet to just cover bottom. Fry on one side until brown and remove from skillet. Repeat with remaining batter.

Filling

1 carton creamed cottage cheese, drained	1 tsp. nutmeg
3/4 c. sugar	1 tsp. vanilla
	Butter

Combine first 4 ingredients and mix well. Place 1 heaping tablespoon cheese filling in center of brown side of each pancake. Fold as for an envelope. Brown in hot butter in blazer pan and place over hot water. Serve with sour cream and jam or fresh fruit. 4 servings.

Mrs. Virginia Kelly, Pass Christian, Mississippi

Freezers are a boon for all today's homemakers — especially those of us who depend on it to help us in planning quick and easy meals. One important clue for successful freezing concerns packaging. Remember that the freezer package must:

>   —*not hold vapor or moisture or the food will dry out.*
>
>   —*be sturdy and able to withstand freezing temperatures.*
>
>   —*be odor free.*
>
>   —*fit the food tightly to prevent darkening and rancidity.*

Meats can be wrapped in freezer paper, aluminum foil, or another wrap which adheres closely. Never freeze or store meat in its original wrapper.

freezer hints

FOR QUICK AND EASY COOKING

Vegetables and fruits pack best in freezer boxes or plastic bags. Most prepared desserts fit in foil or plastic wrap or in bags or boxes made of these materials.

Be careful of seasoning dishes you plan to cook, then freeze. Onion loses its flavor. Garlic, cloves, pimento, and green pepper become stronger after freezing.

There are other tips, too, that homemakers have learned over the years to help them get the most out of their home freezers. A partial listing of the best of these follows:

>   —*Sauces sometimes separate when freezing, especially if they contain a high fat content.*
>
>   —*Diced potatoes will crumble when frozen.*
>
>   —*Salad greens and other leafy vegetables should not be frozen as they lose their crispness.*
>
>   —*Fat becomes rancid about two months after freezing. So, use it sparingly if you plan to freeze cooked food.*
>
>   —*Monosodium glutamate can be added to precooked frozen foods during reheating to bring out their best flavors.*
>
>   —*Most fried foods will lose their crispness when frozen.*
>
>   —*The smaller the pieces of meat you freeze, the more they will dry out while frozen.*

MEASURES, SUBSTITUTIONS, CAN SIZES

For quick and easy measuring and substitutions, consult the following tables:

SUBSTITUTIONS

1 cup whole milk = 1/2 cup of evaporated milk plus 1/2 cup of water or 4 tablespoons of dry whole milk plus 1 cup of water.

1 cup skim milk = 3 to 4 tablespoons of nonfat dry milk plus 1 cup of water.

1 whole egg, for thickening or baking = 2 egg yolks or 2 tablespoons dried whole egg plus 2 1/2 tablespoons water.

1 tablespoon flour, for thickening = 1/2 tablespoon cornstarch, potato starch, or rice starch.

1 cup cake flour, for baking = 7/8 cup all-purpose flour.

1 cup all-purpose flour, for baking breads = up to 1/2 cup bran, whole wheat flour or cornmeal mixed with enough all-purpose flour to fill up cup.

1 teaspoon baking powder = 1/3 teaspoon baking soda plus 1/2 teaspoon cream of tartar.

IN MEASURING, REMEMBER . . .

3 tsp. = 1 tbsp.
2 tbsp. = 1/8 c.
4 tbsp. = 1/4 c.
8 tbsp. = 1/2 c.
12 tbsp. = 3/4 c.
16 tbsp. = 1 c.
5 tbsp. + 1 tsp. = 1/3 c.
4 oz. = 1/2 c.
8 oz. = 1 c.
2 c. fat = 1 lb.
2 c. = 1 pt.

2 c. sugar = 1 lb.
5/8 c. = 1/2 c. + 2 tbsp.
7/8 c. = 3/4 c. + 2 tbsp.
2 2/3 c. powdered sugar = 1 lb.
2 2/3 c. brown sugar = 1 lb.
3 c. sifted flour = 1 lb.
1 lb. butter = 2 c. or 4 sticks
2 pt. = 1 qt.
1 qt. = 4 c.
A few grains = Less than 1/8 tsp.
A pinch is as much as can be taken between tip of finger and thumb.

AVERAGE CAN CONTENTS

1 c.	8 oz.
1 3/4 c.	No. 300
2 c.	No. 1 tall
2 c.	No. 303
2 1/2 c.	No. 2
3 1/2 c.	No. 2 1/2
4 c.	No. 3

INDEX

PHOTOGRAPHY CREDITS: California Strawberry Advisory Board; Rice Council; Turkey Information Service; Olive Administrative Committee; United Fresh Fruit and Vegetable Association; McIlhenny Company; Tuna Research Foundation; Sterno Canned Heat; North American Blueberry Council; American Dairy Association; National Dairy Council; Cling Peach Advisory Board; International Shrimp Council; Pineapple Growers Association; Angostura-Wupperman Corporation; South African Rock Lobster Service Corporation; Pickle Packers International; National Kraut Packers Association; Procter & Gamble Company: Crisco Division; Spanish Green Olive Commission; DIAMOND Walnut Growers, Inc.; Campbell Soup Company; California Avocado Advisory Board; The R. T. French Company; California Prune Advisory Board; Kraft Foods Kitchens; General Foods Kitchens; Evaporated Milk Association; U. S. Department of Commerce: National Marine Fisheries Service; U. S. Trout Farmers Association; McCormick and Company, Inc.; National Livestock and Meat Board; American Home Foods; Processed Apples Institute; Dried Fig Advisory Board; Ocean Spray Cranberries, Inc.; American Dry Milk, Institute, Inc.; Apple Pantry: Washington State Apple Commission.

Printed in the United States of America.